# New Jersey's
# LOST
# Piney Culture

# New Jersey's
## LOST
# Piney Culture

WILLIAM J. LEWIS

THE
History
PRESS

Published by The History Press
Charleston, SC
www.historypress.com

*Front cover, top right*: Courtesy of Jane Gavaghen.

First published 2021

Manufactured in the United States

ISBN 9781467147873

Library of Congress Control Number: 2020944232

# Contents

# Preface

Generally speaking, I never gave much thought to what the definition of a Piney was or wasn't. Growing up, we did what we did at the direction of my dad to help pay the bills and keep food on the table. Pretty much everyone on my dad's side of the family did woods work.

Fast-forward to 2018 to me reading a book about Pineys—John McPhee's *Pine Barrens*. I thought it was a quick and interesting read, but it left out a lot of funny and factual stories that I experienced growing up in the 1980s and 1990s performing "Piney work." Piney work seemed shadowed in a negative way and did not portray the honesty and hardworking ethic of the people who spent their lives in the Pines. Most Piney families highly value putting in a hard day's work. The news that "Piney" was a bad term was a first for me. I thought (maybe naively) a book about the culture and the people in the Pinelands might be better written by one of the people who experienced it firsthand.

During the writing of this book, many interesting things were discovered. Contained in this book are many stories revealing unknown Piney secrets. Like, did you know the Pineys had a direct link to the Philadelphia Mafia and the New York Mafia *other* than what the HBO series *The Sopranos* mentioned in an episode titled "Pine Barrens"? That scene wasn't even shot in the Pines; it was filmed at Harriman State Park in New York.

For the first time, I tell an exclusive story detailing one of the most important families to the Pineys—the Richardsons. I'll bet you never heard of them, and that is why I've dedicated a large portion of this book to their lives (a book within a book). You see, in specifically telling the larger-than-life story of John Richardson, I tell the story of the Reluctant Piney, and even though John "Jack" Richardson is gone from this earth, his children today think of themselves as Pineys and rightly so.

Another oddity is the confession of a Piney mother who describes her alcohol-induced Jersey Devil sighting. Did you know the original Weedman of New Jersey was from Mount Holly, not like that Cheech and Chong funny stuff? What's the MTV series *Jersey Shore*'s connection to a Piney and the continued propagation of that negative stereotype all about? Oh, and another little-known fun fact I bet you didn't know was that Pineys were the first to wear Chuck Taylor Converse shoes, or what the kids today call Chucks. Many of these stories are fading away, as the memories of those few remaining kin to tell the tale of those legends are dwindling.

Along the way, I rediscovered the majestic beauty of being in the Pines that transcends the zip code you're in. Wherever I traveled before, I always noted things that reminded me of home, like a lone pine tree on the slopes of Olomana on the island of Oahu as a young marine stationed in Hawaii, or the size of pinecones in Georgia's "Little Grand Canyon" in Providence Canyon State Park. I quickly realized that I was a Reluctant Piney, and one of the few who witnessed the death of the independent and free Piney culture that came to a close in the early 1990s.

I'd go so far as saying that the Piney culture and lifestyle went the same way by much the same means as the Native American culture—through forced assimilation by the government in the form of state welfare programs and public land acquisition. Other societal ills that affected Native Americans, such as prevalent alcohol abuse and having a different type of education (a "woods degree" rather than society's norm of a high school diploma), became a handicap. Do a quick search on Wikipedia for cultural assimilation and you can see Americans used the lack of education that society deemed best against Native Americans: "Education was viewed as the primary method in the acculturation process for minorities." In the end, much like the Native Americans, Pineys—being a small subset or minority of the New Jersey population—and their knowledge, their "woods degree," was used against them. Now, that generational knowledge bank from the Piney woodsman and the Reluctant Piney is being lost. There are no museums dedicated to preserving the Piney way of subsistence living in the woods.

A Burlington farmer had to point that out to me, as I had not realized it or thought about it in that way. My reluctance to claim the mantra "Proud to be a Piney" came from my family, ending the generations of picking and cutting wild items out of the woods and surrounding farmland. We pulled, picked and cut anything that grew decently in the woods. The last time I picked items that would make someone call me a Piney would have been grapevine wreaths in the summer of 1992. I remember it distinctly; I had just graduated from high school and was working a part-time job at a local grocery store and just started working full time as an ironworker with my dad. I pulled grapevine at an old reliable place where my grandparents and my father had pulled thousands of bales of grapevine before to make an extra buck. The old New Egypt dump was just outside what today we call the Pinelands. I hauled it away in my 1973 Monte Carlo, which, if you're not familiar with that car, had a huge trunk.

In 1993, I joined the Armed Forces, serving as a marine for four years. I left the Piney way behind and never went back to it. If it weren't for a work trip to Florida, I would never have come back to feeling a sense of pride of my origins in the Pines. I'm a birder by hobby, one who seeks out birds, and I enjoy adding new birds to a life list. I traveled across Florida heading east to west from Jacksonville to Gainesville toward a sighting of a vagrant snail kite that was hanging around the city's popular Sweetwater Wetlands Park.

I hiked out to the area just off the wetlands nature trail where it was last seen and ran into a couple from Indiana watching the bird through binoculars. After seeing the bird for myself, a juvenile male snail kite, we engaged in casual conversation and asked each other the usual "Where are you from?" questions. When I said I was from New Jersey, the gentleman told me he had just traveled back from New Jersey a month prior and asked if I ever visited the Pine Barrens. He had always dreamed of taking a trip there after reading John McPhee's book *Pine Barrens*. While he was there, he even bought the Wharton State Forest baseball cap that he was wearing as proof he visited. He was proud to say he explored the Pines.

I had never heard of or thought to read that book before that meeting. After that chance encounter, I did some internet research and found the NJPineBarrens forum, where someone asked the members how to define a Piney and if the word *Piney* was still a derogatory term. This post was dated May 1, 2015. It sparked in me a sort of coming to terms with owning the title "Piney" and acknowledging that there are different types of Pineys today but the old culture of picking pinecones and living off the grid has been phased out by twenty-first-century progress. I want to put an end to the debate about who or what a Piney is and to document the elaborate Piney supply chain that fed the dried floral markets and, hopefully, in the process remove the stigma associated with the name. If you're hearing the term

"Piney" for the first time in this book and already have a neutral impression of what a Piney is, I'd like to ensure that you walk away with a higher and more esteemed opinion of us Pineys. Possibly one day an old Piney will hand this book to his grandkids in hopes of inspiring admiration and pride in their Piney roots.

I have to admit I was pretty disturbed by a person being interviewed when they answered a question on how to describe what a Piney is. This reinforced the need for this book to be written and, to a degree, seek an apology from those in positions of power who had exploited the Pineys in the past. Yes, it was different times, but Piney families still to this day live with the negative stereotypes. No one should tell you that it's wrong to wear the title Piney. No matter what type of Piney you are, we are all part of the same Piney tribe.

Let me end by saying this book isn't just about and for the original settlers of the Pines, even though earlier settlers of the Pines have been mislabeled and negatively characterized and are still owed an apology. This book is also for all those who have lived in or visited the area. The Pinelands Commission reports, "Population of the Pinelands National Reserve—approximately 870,000 by 2010 US Census." Easily one can guess that millions of New Jerseyans and tourists come to the area. This is for those who have hiked, biked, camped or even just driven on one of the many white sandy roads through the Pine Barrens. This book is dedicated to the outsiders always looking in and wanting to belong but never truly being accepted even if they love and respect the place as much as if not more than someone born to the land.

You know the whole mystique of Pineys being hermits and living deep in the woods. They were always a misunderstood lot of outcasts and outsiders, very much relatable with the 1983 movie *Outsiders*, as they were mistreated by their own state and their own communities, not given a chance to live the way they knew best. So, if those few hermits and the Piney families who collected pinecones are gone, then can no one claim the title of "Piney" today?

We know the term has developed and matured into something else. It fits more of the current culture today, but hopefully, I've presented my case on how to redefine the definition to encompass the entire twenty-first-century makeup of the inhabitants of the Pines in 2020 within these pages. By the way, if you're a reader who reads the last page of the book first, like one of my old mentors in the federal government, before diving into the first chapter, you probably will read too much and kill the suspense at the end. But that's okay. Take time to read through the chapters, listening for the main secret in the pile of revealed Piney secrets that is slowly uncovered by the astute reader.

# Acknowledgements

No one can write a book based in historical context without consulting the people who lived it. In the case of the woodsmen and woodswomen of the Pines, there are fewer and fewer of those people to be found with each passing year. I am eternally grateful for those whom I had the chance to interview and consult in the writing of this book. People like Judd "Indian" Cawley, also known as Outlaw, and his mother, Alice Cawley, were living encyclopedias who had real-world experience in the Piney lifestyle that I've tried to document here. Their connected circle of friends became potential interviewees, such as Piney Gordy Lockwood, whose stories that included the Richardson family and the Cawley family were invaluable and provided much-needed content for multiple chapters of the book. My own mother and father, Charlotte and Joseph Lewis, were two more subject matter experts who were able to keep family traditions alive and raise a family on the meager earnings from the woods. Sitting around the kitchen table, I heard many stories that have been captured here. On one of those occasions, my uncle Donald Emery shared his Piney experiences with me as well, and I thank him for it.

Without question, this book could not have been made possible without the sincere efforts of the Richardson family. John Richardson's own son, little Johnny, and daughter Pamela were very supportive of the idea to write the book, and they provided family photographs—often entrusting me with the only copy of many a family album. The artwork in this book undoubtedly conveys the transitioning twenty-first-century Piney, and I am thankful to have worked with some of the best, including Hannah V. Lemke from Little Rock, Arkansas, who did the mixed-media images of the vehicles that will help the reader identify with the various types of today's Pineys, and native South Jerseyan Kristan Barcalow, who hand-drew and painted the Richardson homestead in Wrightstown, New Jersey, from an old family photograph and reproduced from a photo of the Piney Outlaw image.

A Pine Barrens area map was used with permission from Becky Free of the Pinelands Preservation Alliance, and another map of the Mount Holly Fairgrounds was obtained from Art Dubell via a Facebook page titled "The Towns and Villages of the NJ Pinelands." Other historical images of Mount Holly, New Jersey, were obtained by the current and past Mount Holly Historical Society presidents, Lawrence Tigar and Eleanor May (Rhodier) Rich, respectively, both of whom were also interviewed during the research phase of the book and were full of stories and historical footnotes.

Last, but not least, are those who were interviewed and who were my book reviewers in the various stages of the writing process. Subject matter experts in their own fields of study, Thomas Besselmen, Mike Kaliss and Mark Szutarski were supporters and volunteers from Whitesbog Preservation Trust. Author Catherine Antener and administrator of PineyPower.com shared many a Piney story, reviewed the book and shared her personal experiences as a published author, which were invaluable to this would-be writer. My final book reviewer was James Pullaro, a Pinelands amateur historian, whose fact-checking spurred many an idea in the book. Also, a special thanks to many people met along the way at various meeting places that have been there for generations, like Lucille's in Warren Grove and the historical information Diane Brown gave to the project.

I acknowledge all of your contributions and your thoughtful gift(s) to this book project. To my own wife and immediate family, I give special thanks for your willingness to hear my thoughts and logic on many a topic for the book and your brutal honesty when offering unsolicited critique. Another special shout-out to the Facebook groups dedicated to all things Pinelands and especially to my own Facebook group, "Piney Tribe," where a simple comment on a photo turns the gears in my head in a different and better direction. To everyone else who showed kindness and support of the project who I've left off this list, some of whom wanted to remain anonymous, I say a big Piney thank you!

# Introduction

There were a few advance readers who said the background information on the early 1900s Piney was "too dark," and I greatly appreciate that feedback. I feel like they have a more recent image of the Piney that has had the historic treatment romanticized. Now remember, I'm writing this from the perspective of someone who never grew up with the term "Piney," and I had to read in a book that it was a derogatory term to a lot of folks. So, if I get a little passionate in my writing (or too dark), know that it's from the heart.

As you're reading these first few chapters, go ahead and put your feet in the old-time Pineys' shoes. Lace up the shoes, take a few strides and feel how they felt while the state mislabeled them and segregated them from the rest of New Jersey. After all, have you ever wondered why the Parkway didn't go down Route 539, cutting through the Pine Barrens, or why there is no other major interstate highway crisscrossing the Pines? As you go through these chapters, do it with an understanding that you have to know all the bad to appreciate the good, and come away with a new sense of it all. We shouldn't historicize what it is to be a Piney like we as a nation have with the terms "Native American" or "American Indian." "Historicize" a big word for me, so I had to look it up; it means to treat or represent as historical.

You see, to me there is the Hollywood version of what it was to be an American Indian. There is a mystical, romantic image of what it was to be Indian, and somewhere in between is the real truth. I mean, all Native Americans aren't rainbow-wrapped loving couples with feather headdresses, are they? So, for those of you readers who have solid roots in the Piney tribe, this will be old news. To new friends and Pine-dwelling community members, we want you to understand some of the early trials of Pineys that have brought us to today's more prevalent, positive image with the ever-noticeable bumper sticker–toting Pineys: "Proud to be a Piney."

Picture handing your grandkids this book and asking them to read it so that they can better understand the South Jersey culture of the pinewoods. The first few chapters are written not to preach and harp on the early misconceptions of whom and what Pineys were, but they do not gloss over the treatment of Pineys either. Should we forget all the nasty characterizations that the Piney went through? The nefarious book *The Kallikak Family: A Study in the Heredity of Feeble-Mindedness*, from 1912, based on the people of South Jersey and found in many libraries in the New Jersey history section, was written by Dr. Henry Goddard based off field research by his assistant, Elizabeth Kite. She later published her survey findings in 1913, titled *The Pineys*. Their work really popularized for the entire state and the nation that being called a Piney was one of the worst insults, and to get near one was dangerous. The now debunked science behind the Goddard book also was popularized and applied more broadly to American policies that affected not just the people of South Jersey. Think of the ugly scar on American society placed there by the eugenics movement, which was powered by some of the same fake science from the Kallikak study.

Today, it's sometimes politically expedient or politically correct to soften the harshness of historical facts to make things rosier. We should not shy away from the truth. I see what Americans have done to one another, and no matter their skin color, I know it is savagery. But can I not write a book that carries the reader through the tough times to help them gain an understanding of the past wrongs to Pineys and have them come out at the very end being more proud of their heritage or their adopted lifestyle of being a twenty-first-century Piney? Heck, my own children don't know who or what a Piney is, and they certainly don't know who the fictional Kallikak family was or the impact Dr. Goddard and Elizabeth Kite had on the poor rural Piney families of South Jersey. Once you have an inclination to learn about your family history, you want to know the truth—good and bad, not skipping a branch of the tree—so that when you say, "I'm proud to be a [insert surname here]" it means something, right?

One more thing: as I write this paragraph, in the U.S. news media outlets there are discussions on the passed U.S. House Resolution to officially recognize and commemorate the 1915–23 Armenian genocide by the

# NEW JERSEY AWAKES TO ITS DUTIES TOWARD THE "PINEYS"

AFTER a century or more of passing on the other side of the road with averted face the state of New Jersey is going to do something about the "Pineys." It is high time, say investigators, that something be done for and to a colony of poor, ignorant, shack dwelling people whose mental and moral condition is a disgrace to the state.

For a hundred years the tide of civilization has swept past the "Pineys," leaving them stranded in backwaters. Originally of good colonial stock, they are now a shiftless, weak minded, degenerate and immoral race. They dwell in Burlington county, N. J., in the pine country which contains also Lakewood, the famous resort of the wealthy. Sometimes these "Pineys," whose ramshackle houses are passed by the railroad trains and automobiles, are called "pine rats." The name bears testimony to the lack of esteem in which they are held by their respectable neighbors. Their number is estimated at 1,500.

State officials say these neighbors ought to bear part of the blame for the condition of the "Pineys," since they have not done enough to improve the condition of their fellow citizens. You cannot leave a lot of people to live immoral lives by themselves—poor, untaught and neglected, often diseased, with little knowledge of or respect for the marriage relation—without something horrible resulting. Besides, it has been too easy for the "Pineys" to obtain whisky and other strong drink.

The cost has fallen largely on the state. In the "Piney" country one person in every 155 is a public charge, as against the ratio of one in 206 for the entire state. More of the men and women ought to be in asylums and reformatories, say the investigators, instead of being permitted to live together, in and out of wedlock, and continuing to reproduce their own degenerate kind.

The trouble with the "Pineys" is not entirely their poverty, although that is one cause of the misery that is found in their cottages and shacks. The people of the "Pineys" work sometimes at wood chopping, charcoal burning and berry and cranberry picking in season. The money they get for their labor is not enough to give them luxuries, but in connection with the corn and chickens and other simple products which they raise it would afford them livelihoods if it did not go for the whisky that plays so large a part in their lives.

Drink and inbreeding and immoral living have made the "Pineys" a race of moral and mental imbeciles. Many of them are grown men and women with the minds and lack of self control of children. They know no higher law than their own desires, despite the fact that most of them live within easy neighboring distance of farmer folk and village residents who live decent, civilized lives.

Some of the "pine rats" combine with their mental and moral degeneracy a certain shrewdness which teaches them how far they can go in indifference to the law. For instance, they know that the proposed measures for segregating them will be difficult to enforce, in view of the fact that they are not convicted of crime. The men have votes, and their votes have often been manipulated by shrewd and unscrupulous politicians, a factor which complicates the "Piney" problem.

In spite of the laws of the state of New Jersey against bigamy, polygamy and immorality, the "Piney" men and women, and others who are men and women in experience while still children in years, do about as they please. Wives and husbands are exchanged and the former are bought and sold. About the only rule the men seem to regard is the old one that

"They shall take who have the power, And they shall keep who can."

State Charities Commissioner Byers, who has been investigating the "Pineys," said recently:

"They are a pretty good physical type, but utterly lawless morally. Anything like proper respect for legal marriage is unknown to them, but some of the 'Pineys' are beginning to realize their condition. Many of them are in a receptive state of mind. They realize that from the mode of life in the pines, interbreeding and lack of respect for law, there has sprung and is still springing a horde of imbecile, idiotic and criminal children."

BRUCE K. GORDON.

Photos by American Press Association.

**Typical Shack of the "Pineys"—Two of the "Piney" Children.**

*Plainfield Courier News*, July 22, 1913, titled "New Jersey Awakes to Its Duties Toward the 'Pineys.'"

Ottoman Empire. I personally have Armenian friends on social media who, notwithstanding the political motif behind the timing of the resolution, agree that the truth needs to be recognized. This is not to draw equal comparison to what the New Jersey state government did to the people of South Jersey but to express the emotional sense of affirmation the act bestows on those who

John Richardson, circa 1920s, 25 Pine Street, Mount Holly. *Richardson family collection.*

were directly and indirectly affected by the Armenian genocide that killed millions. The Pineys of the past and those living and breathing today deserve an official apology from our state government recognizing the mistreatment of the people of the Pines.

So, what's the mention of a book within a book about, the biography of John Richardson? Richardson's life has only been written about once in one sentence in a 1957 book by Henry C. Shinn titled *The History of Mount Holly*, where Richardson gets sixteen words in print for being the last owner of the Mount Holly Fairgrounds in 1945. As you read the words and pages describing his life, you will better understand the life of a Piney. John's life equaled two sides of the same coin. In telling his life story, we have a love affair, but not your typical one. While a hero to the average Piney of the day, John Richardson did marry a beautiful girl named Helen, but his real obsession was with racehorses and his life's work pioneering Pineycraft floral markets. The dried floral business gave him enough income to hire the best racehorse driver being pulled by the best thoroughbreds, which afforded him a comfortable life—some would say an extravagant lifestyle even through the years of the Great Depression.

I spell out for you the Richardson Calendar at the end of the book in Appendix C, as well as provide you firsthand with life stories of two families who lived the Piney lifestyle working with and for John Richardson. Their lives are very similar to hundreds of other Piney families who worked the woods. There is also in Appendix D a sampling of the five most common items picked by Pineys in a format similar to the second book in the series, *The Richardsons' Piney Calendar: A Field Guide to the Flora of the Pines.* Just like the telling of John Richardson's life story helped illustrate the life of the common everyday Reluctant Piney, telling the tales in those five Pineycraft pages showcases the hardy family traditions and moral code of the Piney in that era.

Chapter 1

# Twentieth-Century Piney Defined

The website of nonprofit 501c3 Pinelands Preservation Alliance (PPA), whose mission it is to help defend the Pine Barrens, states, "The 'Pinelands' is an area of 1.1 million acres designated for special growth management rules. It is one of America's foremost efforts to control growth so that people and the rest of nature can live compatibly, preserving vast stretches of forest, rare species of plants and wildlife, and vulnerable freshwater aquifers." The website Recreation.gov states that the area "includes portions of seven southern New Jersey counties, and encompasses over one-million acres of farms, forests, and wetlands. It contains 56 communities, from hamlets to suburbs, with over 700,000 permanent residents." There is an abundance of great books that have already been written about the land within the Pine Barrens.

And there have been a few noteworthy mentions of the people of the Pines collectively called Pineys. John McPhee, in his epic book *The Pine Barrens*, first printed in 1971, writes, "The Pineys had little fear of their surroundings, from which they drew an adequate living. A yearly cycle evolved that is still practiced, but by no means universally, as it once was." Our storyline also focuses on what the Pineys gathered or picked seasonally in the woods, which mostly came from the area officially recognized as the New Jersey Pinelands National Reserve, Pinelands for short. They may have ventured to overgrown farm fields on the outskirts of the Pine Barrens to gather grasses.

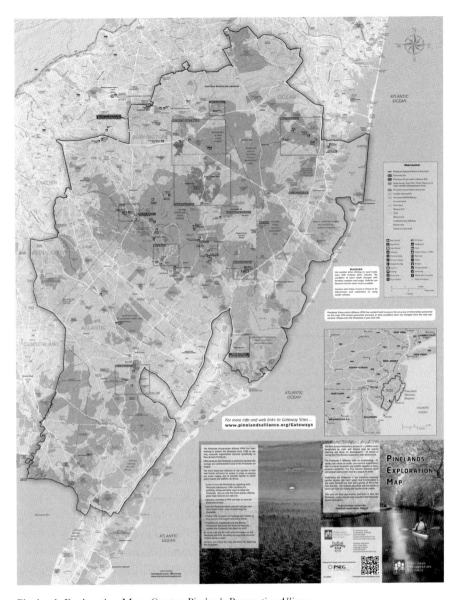

Pinelands Exploration Map. *Courtesy Pinelands Preservation Alliance.*

We introduce to you, the reader, one of the unknown champions of many a Piney family: the Richardsons. This family, and more specifically John Richardson, helped Piney families, mostly poor white families, bring to market(s) the 101 items he supplied to big cities like Philadelphia and New York City. The proximity of the Pine Barrens to those big cities brought many an outsider to the area, and their demand for dried floral goods from the region helped sustain Richardson Wholesale Floral Supply. This then, in turn, continued the opportunity for Pineys to live a subsistence living or, as we more commonly call it today, living off the grid to varying degrees of success into the nineteenth and twentieth centuries.

The life these families lived could be described with the term "working poor," which highlights the importance of local businessmen and businesswomen who helped them supplement their family income by purchasing items foraged from the surrounding lands. Here we need to make a distinction and note that picking and foraging are used interchangeably. By definition, forage refers to an animal, as defined by Merriam-Webster: "food for animals, especially when taken by browsing or grazing." Pineys living off the substance of the land foraged for berries and plants for personal use but regularly "picked" items to sell to wholesale dry florists for much-needed income and quick cash.

But what is a Piney? A recurring theme is that Pineys were very private people who often lived simple lives with little modern conveniences. Some would say they were very poor, but that's by modern standards. Families lived out their lives for generations never traveling out of state and never having left the country. One of my interview questions was what defines a Piney. A friend of many a Piney and outsider of sorts, Johnny Richardson described a Piney as "a person that came from Chatsworth, Browns Mills, Warren Grove areas in the pines. They were adverse to 40 hour normal work weeks. Some were on government assistance and many were known to overindulge in alcohol but all were very honest people. They weren't materialistic and or schooled but weren't stupid either. They could build and be very mechanical." Even though they didn't have ordinary 9-to-5 jobs, they put in more than forty hours in a week. This was possibly a leftover trait coming from stock that was used to performing twelve- to fourteen-hour workdays in past Pinelands industries like paper, coal, bog iron and farming. Johnny pulled his definition from a lifetime of intimate involvement with the hundreds of Piney families who were supported by his dad's business.

Speaking from experience, a neighboring farmer to the Richardsons said of the olden times Piney, "The most independent and free people that there ever were in this country that worked in an environment that was very challenging and…they were independent which learned a trade that was passed on by generation to generation. It didn't fail they weren't there with their hand out. They weren't there that needed welfare." Their fiercely independent nature was due to the remoteness of living in the Pines and having the ability and smarts to adapt to their surroundings. A farmer is tied to the land, and that may have influenced the farmer's definition of a Piney in that he admired their independence and ability to sustain their way of living not off one set plot of land but the entire Pine Barrens and surrounding open space. But farmers and Pineys were cut from the same cloth. After all, the Reluctant Piney was a farmer but without land, as he got up every morning and went out to harvest the Pineycraft crops that were available and in season—even though, for example, it wasn't a guarantee that last year's location of buttons was going to be as good as it was the year before, so they had to keep their eyes on the woods' picking locations.

Even our federal government wanted to clearly define what a Piney was. The American Folklife Center at the Library of Congress in Washington, D.C., spent four years trying to capture the Piney way of life. The Pinelands Folklife Project was conducted from May 1983 to September 1986 to do just that. I caught up with Dennis McDonald, one of the photojournalists who was contracted to take photos for the Pinelands Folklife Project and author of such titles as *Medford* (Images of America) and *Smithville*. When asked about the general feeling and mission of the Pinelands Folklife Project, he stated, "People had an idea of the Pines mostly from the outsiders. Just being a barren landscape between Philadelphia and the Shore. Yes, there were trees, yes, there were sand roads, but beyond that you know I don't think anyone really knew what went on there and what was the big deal about making it a National Reserve. That seemed odd to people, that it was a bunch of land with nobody in it. The reality was a lot different. People made their living off of a lot of the places in the Pines, as shown in the book. I think they even tried to demonstrate that the culture of the Pines was something that went back generation after generation after generation and was unique to that area." This was a lofty idea to document the life of the people in the Pines who were multidimensional and at times difficult to find.

This excerpt from the monumental Pinelands Folklife Project's *One Space, Many Places*, printed in 1986, brings us closer to defining what a Piney is or was:

> *Cultural journalists often romanticize Pineys as indigenous, reclusive people who gather pinecones and other native plant materials for a living. Although the gatherers are, in fact, satisfying a very modern demand for the materials in the florist market they are erroneously associated in the public mind with subsistence lifestyles in earlier phases of civilization. For some consumers and purveyors of the region's folklore, gatherers comprise*

*the undiluted essence of "Pineyness." Notions of what and who Pineys are comprise a sizeable body of folklore in itself. One woman, a Medford resident, held that Pineys—among whom she does not include lumberers, trappers, farmers, or recently arrived ethnic groups—are the only fitting subject for folklife documentation. Her opinion is reinforced by formulaic presentations of Pine Barrens folklore: Men and women who give lectures on the folklore of the Pine Barrens, they show a pile of pinecones, people who come in with sacks on their backs of things they've collected. That, to me, would be what you would be after. That's Piney culture because it's gone on for centuries. (Interview, Mary Hufford and Sue Samuelson, November 13, 1983. AMH021)*

After years of personal interactions during photoshoots on assignment with the Pinelands Folklife Project, Dennis McDonald suggests a Piney is "someone who made their living off the woods or off the land in the Pine Barrens area. It could be a carver, a farmer, a trapper, any one of the numerous amounts of things. To go beyond that, there are lots of people that I would consider that are Pineys that just love the Pines. They're nothing more than that. It's hard to say exactly what a Piney would be, but it's certainly someone that loves the land probably the number one definition. Unbelievable love of that lifestyle, that land and that resource that we all love to be in." Two great books were spurred from the key people on the Pinelands Folklife Project: *One Space, Many Places* by Mary Hufford and *Pinelands Folklife*, edited by Rita Zorn Moonsammy, David Steven Cohen and Lorraine E. Williams.

In her 1983 PhD dissertation "A Psycho-Social Impact Analysis of Environmental Change in the New Jersey Pine Barrens," Nora Rubinstein eloquently outlined Pineyness:

*Pineyness was based on geographical location at various stages in life, with birth-place being of greatest significance, [then] ancestry, age, occupation, economic status, family ties, and an amorphous quality many comprehend, but few can determine. It is an attitude, a way of being in the world, an essence or quality not included in the legislative description.... [My] search for the elusive Piney has come full circle, from geography and language, ancestry and occupation to an affective sense—a feeling for family, but most important, for the land, for the experience of "being" in the Pines. It is just over the horizon or as Janice Sherwood said, "a little deeper in the woods than you are."*

She tells of being a Piney by your sense of attitude and your love of the Pine Barrens. With Rubinstein's outline, we come closer to the answer of what a Piney is. It's that "attitude" part of the description that everyone struggles to define.

This theme of intangible feeling and attitude defining Pineyness is echoed in a book used in collegiate planning courses in New Jersey titled *Water, Earth, and Fire* by Jonathan Berger and John W. Stinton. They go on to use the term *topophilia*, or

> *the attachment to physical places—cemeteries, cedar forests, rivers and lakes, bays, and the old home place. While there is a good deal of mobility in and out of the Pines, those who leave for jobs in the city or a dream farm in Maine return often. It is true that people return to, or even decide to stay in, the Pine Barrens for family reasons, but love of the physical setting in which they grew up plays a major role. There are many residents of the Pines who grew up in some other place but after falling in love with the Pine Barrens came to live in them.*

More than anything, the love of the land—that million-plus acres of woods first described as desolate—and that "attitude" mentioned earlier as fiercely independent define what a Piney was and is today. In that loving embrace, the people of the Pines relish in the toughness and the endowments of the land. The remoteness of the Pines brings out the best in them, and the seasonal gifts Mother Earth bestows upon them nourish them year after year.

Chapter 2

# Is "Piney" Still a Bad Word?

An anonymous South Jersey farmer spoke about how the generations before the twentieth-century Pineys were more independent and lived a truer life off the land in the Pines. Up until, say, the early 1900s, the Piney way of life depended on hunting, fishing, trapping and harvesting items to supplement the family budget, creating an independence from a modern New Jersey forty-hour workweek their descendants do not enjoy.

On June 28, 1913, Governor James Fielder called Pineys "NJ degenerates." The governor came out publicly against the people of the region and, ultimately, the Piney way of life all based on lies published in a report by Dr. Henry Goddard and Elizabeth Kite, which had serious ramifications on the Pineys back then and still has effects that continue to be felt to this day. While Governor Fielder used his words and position of power to tear down an entire culture as a plank in his reelection platform, it was John McPhee who ultimately helped save the Pineys with his words, which produced the power to influence a positive change.

The Kite report described the Pineys as inbred heathens. As a result, many state government policies and local government actions were taken against the Piney people, and the Piney world was turned upside down during this time. The New Lisbon Development Center was established in 1914 in the heart of the Pines. Two years later, the Burlington County Colony for Feeble-Minded Boys, which was formerly a branch for the Training School at Vineland also located at New Lisbon, was turned over to the state. Author Robert McGarvey described the times nicely: "The psycho business in the area boomed."

New state-funded mental wards were established in Burlington County, and both new and old facilities saw an increase in such wards. An excerpt from the *Batsto Citizens Gazette* read, "The towns and cities had just as many degenerates and feebleminded. There were over 12,300 wards of the State in 1913. The sparsely populated Pinelands probably provided but a fraction of the inmates, but because of their isolation it had been easier to single them out for research."

Burlington County, the largest county in the state by area, also had the highest proportion of state wards to population. Having been painted as a culture of people who could not avoid their condition because it was hereditary and all-encompassing, the residents of the South Jersey Pine Barrens became even more withdrawn from the public eye, and the Pineys became even more reclusive in nature and suspicious of outsiders. While the science had been refuted by numerous colleagues of Dr. Goddard and Kite and by other experts in the scientific community several times over— Goddard's study was found to be riddled with false documentation and based on false assumptions that have since been proven wrong—the public condemnation that initially followed the report's publication is, arguably, the greatest catalyst to the end of the subsistence-living lifestyle of the people of the Pine Barrens and the ultimate extinction of that mold of Piney.

In 1913, researcher Elizabeth Kite published her explosive report, titled *The Pineys*, that included "tales of heavy drinking, livestock quartered in children's bedrooms, incest and widespread inbreeding." The report caused quite a scandal in New Jersey. Governor James T. Fielder made a personal visit to the Pine Barrens, where he found the residents to be "a serious menace" to the public. He stated, "They have inbred, and led lawless and scandalous lives, till they have become a race of imbeciles, criminals and defectives." Following this visit, he asked the legislature to isolate the area from the rest of the state.

The most infamous Piney who ever lived is Deborah Kallikak. While she herself has been all but forgotten, the Goddard and Kite caricature of her and her Piney roots lives on in the minds of outsiders to the region today. Sadly, the label is still brandished like a red-hot iron cow prod and negatively applied to most residents of South Jersey. The myth that the people of the Pines are inbred, heathens and to be avoided or watched with a close eye but at a far distance when encountered derived from the Kite report and continues to be spread by outsiders.

It wasn't until the 1985 seminal work *Minds Made Feeble: The Myth and Legacy of the Kallikaks*, by Dr. David John Smith, that once and for all Deborah and

the public image of a Piney were restored in good form, even though we still see the Goddard myth today in 2020. In his book, Dr. Smith stated, "I have attempted to describe the making of a social myth and to illustrate how lives were restricted, damaged, and even destroyed as a result of that myth. In the process of researching and writing it, I have been reminded of, and made more sensitive to, how careful we must be in the sciences and in human service professions about the myths that we accept, foster, or even create. Myths have a way of becoming reality. Myths have a way of gathering force as they are passed along. They have a way of surviving the intent and lifetime of their creators."

During the various interviews that were conducted for this book, no one could recollect what was published by Dr. Smith and whether it helped at all in lifting the black cloud from the term "Piney." Did the young Kallikak girl, who was admitted to the Vineland training school in 1897 at the age of eight, even know her own birth name? Her story is so tragic that it could be a Hollywood movie. She lived in state custody until she died in 1978. The actions of a few who "drank the Kool-Aid" poured by Goddard and Kite fully believed that Deborah inherited her intellect—or lack of one—from her mother and that although she exhibited many normal behaviors, her life behind the walls of a sanatorium was justified to keep her from continuing the line of imbeciles and further plaguing the state of New Jersey. This lifelong captivity is a shameful chapter in Piney history.

In Dr. Smith's book, he stated:

> *Deborah Kallikak was considered to be "feebleminded." More specifically, she had been classified as a moron, a designation that Goddard had coined from a Greek word meaning foolish. The label moron came to be widely applied to people who were considered to be "high grade defectives"—those who were not retarded seriously enough to be obvious to the casual observer and who had not been brain-damaged by disease or injury. Morons were characterized as being intellectually dull, socially inadequate, and morally deficient. From the beginning of his research, Goddard was inclined to believe that these traits were hereditary in origin. He was of the opinion that reproduction among people with these traits posed a threat to the social order and the advancement of civilization.*

How in the world could science condemn a human condition based on either so little evidence or the incorrect evidence of one Dr. Goddard and one field assistant, Elizabeth Kite—especially when their "research" stemmed from a supposedly "defective" Piney family, the Kallikaks, which rapidly ushered in the sterilization and the eugenics movement in America? Dr. Smith wrote, "The aim of the eugenics movement was to conduct hereditary research that would result in the upgrading of the human stock, similar to the way genetics was being applied in agriculture and animal husbandry. People with superior traits were to be encouraged to reproduce early and often. People with defective characteristics were to be prohibited from reproduction." Eugenics is arguably one of America's darkest, best-kept secrets. The eugenics movement utilized the popularization of the study performed on the fictional Kallikak family and Deborah Kallikak. Dr. Goddard used his platform to influence and eventually institute his scientific method at Ellis Island, which led to the 1924 Immigration Restriction Act, which banned eastern European immigrants—Russians, Italians, Hungarians and Jews—based on the Binet test or mental intelligence test.

Multiple books have been written to disprove the theory of Dr. Goddard and to showcase how he doctored photographs to show menacing faces on the Kallikak family and that the feebleminded ancestral tree wasn't based on any factual data. Dr. Smith wondered how,

> in view of the easily apparent flaws in the Kallikak study, and its rejection in authoritative circles for many years, it has continued to be given such strong credence and to find such warm support in many quarters? The answer is a simple one. As suggested previously, there are persons everywhere who relish the thought that some groups, races, classes or strains (always including the ones to which they themselves belong) are born to be superior and dominant, and that other groups are destined by nature to be inferior and subordinate. Thus, the Kallikak study when it appeared was eagerly welcomed because it apparently offered "scientific proof" that a high proportion of the social and physical ills of mankind were directly or indirectly due to hereditary defects, and that these could be eliminated most effectively and a super race speedily produced, by breeding out the "unfit."

That's why many people, even today in the twenty-first century, are still propagating the Goddard caricature of Deborah Kallikak, whose shadow still casts a negative stereotype of what a Piney is or isn't.

Chapter 3

# The Largest Nail in the Reluctant Piney's Coffin

## THE CULTURE OF PRESERVATION

Similarities can be drawn to another indigenous people of the Pines and their subsequent plight. Before there were Pineys, there were Native American Lenni-Lenape who lived in the Pines. In his 1980 book *Down Barnegat Bay: A Nor'easter Midnight Reader*, Robert Jahn writes, "Although the Lenni-Lenape were once a flourishing culture believed to number more than 10,000 before the coming of the Europeans, by 1775 less than 200 Indians remained in South Jersey. Most Lenni-Lenape left the state in 1802 to reunite with other tribes in New York."

As more and more early European settlers learned to adapt to the barren lands of South Jersey, more and more pressure and outright violence was applied to the Natives. Jahn wrote, "Although local Indians legally signed away the rights to their lands, most of them didn't fully understand the meaning of private property, and sometimes conflicts arose with the settlers when Indians persisted in returning to their old fishing and hunting grounds. According to Alfred Hulse, an Osbornville old-timer, six of the last Lenni-Lenape around Metedeconk were lynched in the 1850's by an angry white mob because the Indians refused to stay away."

One of the reasons the Lenni-Lenape left South Jersey was because the remaining space they had been sequestered to could not sustain their way of life. It might have been karma, it might have been bad luck coming back to the early settlers of the region, but a similar pressure would be applied to the traditional Piney type, known as the Reluctant Piney (those who collected pinecones and other Pineycraft items). They went all but extinct in the mid- to late 1900s.

In 1905, the state created its first state forest park in the area—Bass River. Open spaces were critical to Pineys, who for generations went back to the same location to gather pinecones, birch, sphagnum moss and other items. The Lenni-Lenape had gathered many of the same items, using them for food and medicinal purposes. We know that the local Native Americans had taught many of the first European settlers how to survive and prosper in their new home. In Cecil Still's book *Botany and Healing: Medical Plants of New Jersey and the Region*, he states, "When European explorers and settlers came to North America, their survival often depended on native American knowledge—freely shared—of plants unfamiliar to the foreigners." Cecil Still is a descendant of the most famous African American Piney and Pinelands doctor, James Still (1812–1885). Cecil tells of Benjamin Smith Barton, who studied with the Native Americans in Western Pennsylvania and posthumously published his work *Collections for an Essay towards a Materia Medica of the United States*. Barton described the locals as "native Americans— then often called 'doctors of instinct.'" It's no surprise that the items the Pineys collected for use in floral crafts, such as cattails, can also be eaten or used medicinally. The Richardson Calendar—named after John Richardson, who pioneered and dominated the Pineycraft market—consisted of over one hundred items that grew in the Pine Barrens area. The intimate knowledge of many of the Pineycraft items contained in the Richardson Calendar has been in the American lexicon since precolonial days.

As these lands became closed off to the Pineys, their way of life became threatened. The people of New Jersey gradually saw a paradigm shift from natural resource exploitation to conservation. Various groups of people and governmental bodies influenced the culture of preservation we see today. Once a piece of land is preserved, it becomes illegal to cut or collect plants without a permit. Now the region's forests are best described as postindustrial forest.

It is as if the words of W.F. Mayer, printed in the May 1859 *Atlantic Monthly*, were coming to fruition:

> *We shall not suffer his company much longer in this world—poor, neglected, pitiable, darkened soul that he is this fellow-citizen of ours. He must move on; for civilization, like a stern, prosaic policeman, will have no idlers in the past. There must be no vagrants, not even in the forest....We must have farms here, and happy homesteads, and orchards...instead of silent aisles and avenues of mournful pine-trees, sheltering such forlorn miscreations as our poor cranberry-stealing friends! There is no room for a gypsy in all our*

*wide America! The* [Pine] *Rat must follow the Indian—must fade like breath from a windowpane in winter!*

Obviously, there were negative feelings toward Pineys prior to the Goddard report and the theatrics of Governor James Fielder in June 1913. More and more open land disappeared. Typical examples of Piney dwellings were homesteads with or without electricity, out in the middle of a forest, down one of those long white sandy dirt roads. Gordy Lockwood, a self-professed Piney, said he'd rather live without electricity and be in the woods. Like the Native Americans, Pineys lived a life in tune with the land, and as such, their way of life was more in sync with the forests.

At the northern end of what we call the Pinelands today sits a block of federally owned property. In 1917, the U.S. government established a military base at that northern terminus due to the need to train U.S. soldiers for the warfront in Europe and the U.S. entrance into World War I. Today, that site is known as Joint Base McGuire-Dix-Lakehurst and is forty-two thousand contiguous acres. As the base grew, many Piney families were moved out of their hermit-like homesteads. It is interesting to note that pine pulpwood, cut in four-foot lengths and used to make paper, was removed to make way for the military bases. Some said the trees were sixty to seventy-five feet in height. The Pineys were used as laborers to cut the pulpwood, and they also collected the pinecones at the tops of these trees once they were harvested.

Some nine years later in nearby Jackson Township, the state established the first forest tree nursery in 1926. Then, in 1955, one of the largest blocks of land in the Central Pine Barrens—which was privately held by the Wharton Estate—became a state park. Jonathan Berger highlights the history of the acquisition nicely in his book *Water, Earth, and Fire*:

> *In 1915 Wharton heirs offered the state of NJ all of 100,000 acres to the state which put it to a vote. Voters defeated the question 123,995 to 103,456 with almost all South Jersey voting against the state's purchase. In 1950 New Jersey did purchase the tract, almost 2 percent of the state's total land area, for over $3 million (Pierce 1964). Wharton had made himself popular with many local residents. He was personally courteous, his projects provided local employment, and he allowed local use of his extensive lands for hunting, trapping, gathering, and fishing. Further, his ownership continued the century-long pattern of plantation ownership by prestigious Philadelphia families and well-known local managers. Public ownership promised none of the benefits of Wharton's ownership and all*

*of the drawbacks. Local residents believed in gainful employment based on local resources; this work was their life. Public ownership meant an end to this pattern and another form of outside control. It was never clear that public ownership served the best interests of local people, and it still is not.*

So, basically, the entire 100,000-acre Wharton Tract became off-limits to the Pineys, who had previously collected pinecones, sweethuck and other items in the area that they then sold to the dried floral markets. The Division of Fish and Wildlife (DFW) law below describes the Piney pickings on state lands as being unlawful. In personal correspondence with a representative of the DFW, it was stated, "The Current 7:25-2.1 was adopted on August 15, 1983, but there was definitely a no-cutting rule prior to 1969 because in the 1983 rulemaking, there was no mention of a prior NJ Register published rule. This means that the first 'rule' to have no cutting was prior to the creation of the NJ Register in 1969."

*§ 7:25-2.1 Cutting or Damaging Vegetation*
*No person or persons shall at any time cut, fell, dig up, pull up, damage, gather, carry away, take, remove or destroy any tree, shrub, vine or other vegetation or part thereof without written permission or other authorization of the Division. Nothing in this section shall apply to public utility companies or their agents engaged in the maintenance of existing utility company rights of way, provided that prior notice is given to the Division.*

Rules and regulations were loosely enforced in the early days, and Pineys were still able to pick items off public property. John McPhee's book *The Pine Barrens* stirred the public's conscience and assembled an army of environmentalists to protect the Pine Barrens, driving the creation in 1978 of the Pinelands National Reserve. The authoritative body Pinelands Commission is a state agency created to safeguard the Pinelands National Reserve, drawing from laws passed at both the state and federal levels. Congress passed the National Parks and Recreation Act in 1978, followed by the New Jersey state legislature passing the Pinelands Protection Act (PPA) in 1979. The PPA gave the newly created Pinelands Commission time to enact a regulatory structure to benefit development and preservation in the form of the Comprehensive Management Plan (CMP).

But all of this was a double-edged sword for Pineys. Business demand for natural dried floral items was at an all-time high when McPhee's book was published, which, as a nationally syndicated print, fueled increased

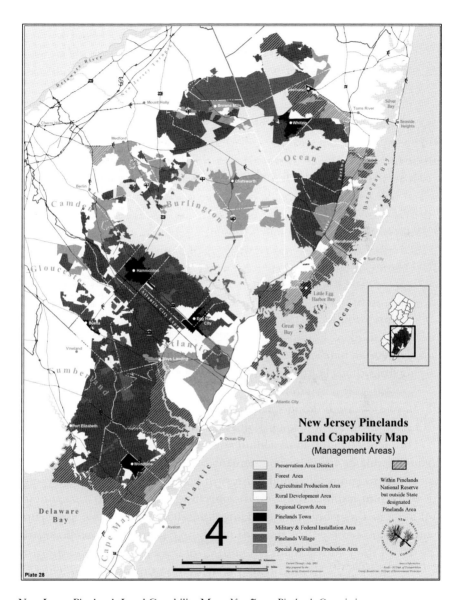

New Jersey Pinelands Land Capability Map. *New Jersey Pinelands Commission.*

demand for Pine Barrens–related goods. Whereas before the state no-cutting regulations were, at best, inconsistently enforced at local levels, after McPhee's book the laws were strictly enforced across the board at the federal, state and local levels, and many Pineys began to get tickets for criminal trespassing and illegal cutting.

The first of its kind, the New Jersey Pinelands National Reserve—a United States Federal Reserve managed and governed by the State of New Jersey and which carried with it laws forbidding the collection of natural items—pushed many Piney families to either maintain their lifestyle and break the law or finally submit to societal demands and transition to a "new normal" forty-hour workweek. At the heart of the CMP was the Preservation Area District, composed of some 295,000 acres right smack in the middle of Piney picking territory. This area was critically important to pickers who cut most if not all of the seasonal items that went to dried floral markets in towns such as Chatsworth and Lower Bank.

It wasn't just the military bases or parks and recreation that removed open, harvestable lands to the Piney gatherers. When the New Jersey Turnpike opened in 1951, it consumed huge swaths of land in South Jersey. Partially man-made firestorms destroyed hundreds of acres in the southern area as well. The town of Chatsworth saw fires in 1954. In 1963, the largest wildfire burned nearly 190,000 acres of Pinelands. Again in 1965, this time due to a local policeman/arsonist, the Pine Barrens burned at various sites; in total, sixty-nine fires were attributed to this person. In fact, the Pinelands Reserve has been under continuous pressure since the creation of the Pinelands Commission in 1979 from the development of both industry and public housing.

Multiple factors pressing in on the Piney hunter/gatherers ultimately broke the generational cycle of picking and gathering items from the Pines in the late 1970s. Pineys continued to work and collect items on the outskirts of towns. In areas that were considered waste areas or disturbed areas—like public right-of-way areas such as a power line or an abandoned sand pit—many of the plants they cut could still be gathered. But if they found those same plants on state or private land, they had to ask themselves if taking the chance to cut the Pineycraft item was worth the risk of breaking the law.

Pinelands National Reserve (PNR). *Author's collection.*

When talking about this very topic during a 2020 interview with Piney Bill Wasiowich, whom John McPhee wrote about in *The Pine Barrens*, Bill echoed those same sentiments: "I can show one place after another where I pulled sphagnum moss. There ain't no way you're going to get in there. Yeah, they blocked the road off or got their no trespassing signs tacked up there. You can't go nowhere; you're out of business." There is a treasure-trove of stories of the resistant Piney families who turned to "outlawing," a common term for cutting plants illegally on state property or killing deer out of season. The outlaw mantle had been worn by many Piney characters in the past, including British Loyalists who were said to rob stagecoaches and privateers, who ransacked British ships and sailed them up the Mullica River. In the end, even this type of "Pineyness" succumbed to progress in the early 1990s, thus severing the seasonal connection of those woods Pineys.

We have to be careful as a society when we rush in to protect something that we don't "trample the essence" of what makes it so special to warrant the protection in the first place. The balance of nature and nurture early on in the conservation effort is critical. We failed the Pineys of the nineteenth century like we failed the Native American tribes of New Jersey.

The Pinelands National Reserve crosses into multiple counties: Atlantic, Burlington, Camden, Cape May, Cumberland, Gloucester and Ocean. Future Open Space and land conservation by the various entities within the state will ensure this list grows larger than the current snapshot.

## WILDLIFE MANAGEMENT AREAS

| | |
|---|---|
| Colliers Mills | Great Bay Boulevard |
| Greenwood Forest | Tuckahoe |
| Stafford Forge | Peaslee |

Colliers Mills Wildlife Management Area. *Author's collection.*

Maple Lake

Dennis Creek

Beaver Swamp

Heislerville

Make Peace Lake

Winslow

White Oak Branch

Hammonton Creek

Wading River

Swan Bay

Port Republic

Absecon

Forked River Mountain

Manchester

Whiting

Upper Barnegat Bay

Manahawkin

# REFUGES

Edwin B. Forsythe National Wildlife Refuge

Cape May National Wildlife Refuge

Woodford Cedar Run Wildlife Refuge

Unexpected Wildlife Refuge

# STATE FORESTS

Wharton

Brendan T. Byrne

Bass River

Belleplain

Penn

Island Beach

# COUNTY PARKS

Wells Mills

Estell Manor

Cattus Island

Cloverdale Farm

Jakes Branch

*Top*: Edwin B. Forsythe National Wildlife Refuge. *Author's collection.*

*Middle*: Brendan T. Byrne State Forest. *Author's collection.*

*Bottom*: Wells Mills Ocean County Park. *Author's collection.*

# STATE PARKS

Double Trouble
Forest Resource Education Center (FREC)

# PRESERVES

El Dora Nature
Maurice River
Dennis
Lizard Tail Swamp
Dorothy
Penny Pot
Turtle Creek

Forked River
Crossley
Evert
North Branch
Michael Huber Prairie Warbler
Franklin Parker

*Top*: Forest Resource Education Center (FREC). *Author's collection.*

*Bottom*: Dot and Brooks Evert Trail Preserve. *Author's collection.*

Chapter 4

# *Are Pineys Environmental Heroes?*

Even though Joseph Wharton amassed over 100,000 acres in the Pines, when he owned the land, the local Pineys were still able to cut and gather the traditional dried floral items they sold to markets. For years and years, the Pineys went back to the same locations to cut and pick items—places like the Plains for pinecones, Medford Lakes for birch, Lower Bank for cattails, Chatsworth Bogs for buttons and elkshorn and Tuckerton for sea statice. Some years the plants they gathered didn't come up as thick as the year before, but most of the time once they cut an item it came back the following year. Old-timers would say, "Thicker than the hair on a dog." Items regenerated or were picked in low-quality habitat. When items were properly harvested, it was sort of like pruning a backyard tree, which helps to maintain the health of some of the plants and trees found in the Pines. So as they saw it, when the state made them into outlaws for picking items that they used to regularly cut, they saw no sense in it.

You'd cut birch in an area and it would grow back twice as good for next year's picking. If you picked grapevine for wreaths and pulled every piece of grapevine in that specific area, it would make room for younger grapevine that would grow back twice as nice as before. Pinecones were no different. Dozens of families picked off the Plains, and every year there were plenty of cones to pick. Just ask one of the last old-timey Pineys, Mr. Bill Wasiowich. In a recent interview in 2020, he stated, "For pinecones it definitely does improve the place out there. It must prune them and all. If you pick them out there and you got a bad spot and start picking them about two or three years, you start to notice the cones getting a little more thicker out there and of higher quality pinecones." The same area year after year was used to cut cattails. The wild grasses like pepper grass and pennycress grew in disturbed areas that were left fallow by local farmers. Farmers were okay with the Pineys collecting the grasses, for as far as they were concerned the grasses were weeds. Earlier farmers in New Jersey and parts of South Jersey had the luxury of an abundance of land to farm where they could keep certain fields left unseeded. With New Jersey living up to its title as the most densely populated state, farm size has been greatly reduced and modern farming technology has enabled some farmers to make their landholding more productive and less likely to have a field unplanted for a season. But if the field was left fallow long enough, another beautiful yield of grasses could be hand pulled and sold to market.

These locations or patches that the Pineys went back to year after year were handed down through the generations. A father would teach a son where to find the best place and time to collect elkshorn, aka gold crest, so that it could be sold to the flower markets just like his father had shared with him. Holistically, the Piney was more connected to the land than outsiders were. Pineys were capable of noting that the second wave of pepper grass was taking root in the old fallow farm field in July, green plume grass heads were just starting to show in August (not the harvesting purple color yet), the false buttons that came up in June would be followed by the true picking buttons or ten-angled pipewort but not until August and the local white pine trees were loaded with new cones, and come a good fall wind, the harvest could begin. They associated particular species of plants like heather as an indicator of an old homestead's presence, being that it grew in disturbed sandy soil. They had a high degree of environmental awareness or aptitude. And these dried floral items meant to go into a dried floral arrangement for home and business décor were far the better choice than decorating with plastic flowers or imported dry flowers, as the carbon footprint for that supply chain had to be far worse than what the local Piney spent harvesting. And while not a key environmental factor but more of a positive economic boost, the money earned helped them sustain their lifestyle and was put back into the local economy, whereas buying an imported bunch of cattails did not provide the same benefit.

Outsiders like plant hobbyists and botanists benefited from their generational wisdom too. They sought out local Pineys to assist in locating unique Pinelands flora and fauna. The most famous of this guide-type work was when Pineys assisted the creator of the modern-day blueberry, Elizabeth White, at Whitesbog Village in Browns Mills, New Jersey. From *Pinelands Folklife*: "She devised a pay scale for bushes bearing fruit that would not fall through the 5/8th inch hole in her blueberry gauge, and she named the bushes after their finders: Rube Leek of Chatsworth found a bush. I did not know it was anything special at that time." "The Rubel has been the keystone of blueberry breeding." To think we would not have that blue ball of deliciousness that provides antioxidants and vitamin C if it wasn't for those early Pineys who knew the best places to find blueberry bushes. Blueberry farmers still to this day use the Rubel blueberry bush to grow commercial blueberries.

Along with the applied collecting lessons were lessons on how to be good stewards of the land. Is it a far stretch to say that many of the early Pineys were eco-warriors? It didn't make sense to illegally dump your trash on a road or tear up a road 4x4ing that you would use to get to an old forgotten cranberry bog that was a goldmine for what you would be collecting next season. Many a Piney carried a shovel to fill in ruts to make their next trip down that old road that much easier. It might have been born out of necessity, but the woods people took very good care of a lot of the Pines. Also when out scouting the woods for Pineycraft items, they were resourceful enough to be the ultimate recyclers. If they found glass bottle dumps in the Pines, there was money to be had for those who collected the bottles and took them to the junkyard. And many old vehicles or old abandoned steel farm equipment were left in the woods; in some instances Pineys would haul them to a junkyard as an additional source of income. They did litter patrol before it was a mainstream thing to do.

Many of these Reluctant Pineys or Woods Pineys who still worked the Richardson Calendar also spent considerable time in the woods hunting, fishing and trapping. Some city slicker hunters had to put ribbons up to remind them of the path, but Pineys usually didn't use ribbons. They had a breadth of knowledge of the woods and the paths that they personally made into them. The paths might lead to a deer stand or might lead to a great spot to cut hogbrush or sweethuck. Pineys were early adopters of "leave no trace." Besides the knowledge of the woods, they also had a tendency to not want to share their spots. Places nicknamed Goldmine, where a Pineycraft item was found in large quantities, wasn't something you wanted other Pineys to find. There were other Pineys out there looking to make a quick dollar too. So you kept your honey wells to yourself. In the process, you didn't announce to the world that you've marked your trail with blaze pink ribbons so come take a look. And the woods remained a pristine image like on the back of a U.S. stamp.

Early on, the Pineys saw the environmental indicators that the landscape was changing. When not collecting cattails out in the meadows, those who trapped checked their muskrat traps in those same meadows. The muskrat is an omnivore, and its diet is dependent on cattails. Likewise, the Piney was also dependent on cattails during the cattail cutting season from Memorial Day to the second week of June. Note the cattail meadows had no apex predators and muskrat trappers were helping control the population, which, if left unchecked, could destroy whole stands of cattails and open up a large area for invasive species like purple loosestrife and phragmites, which plague the riverbanks today, to move in. Piney trappers who could get five dollars per pelt remember collecting thousands of muskrats before the invasive plant phragmites (aka plume grass) took over the fields of cattails. You have the proverbial canary in the coal mine—extinction of cattails by an invasive plant, an indicator that the natural landscape changed forever for those brackish meadows.

Again, these fiercely independent people were on to something with their simple lifestyle, living a no-frills, no-wants life. They were resourceful enough to work certain months of the year following the Richardson Calendar while they spent other months hunting and fishing to sustain their lives. It's almost unheard of to see a Piney family being materialistic. All that was needed was a beat-up vehicle to get down those sandy, sugary white pine roads to haul out the day's Pineycraft load and a home, preferably tucked deep within the pines. Their preferred lifestyle is reminiscent of the TV family the Waltons based in the Blue Ridge Mountains of Virginia. This simpler lifestyle required few manufactured goods and created little waste. Not all Pineys lived this way, but it was almost a community norm. Today's twenty-first-century environmental heroes preach the ills of societal hoarding and overconsumption without regard to the environment. I think we all can agree that the Piney lifestyle is more in tune with nature and very detached from the nation's quest in keeping up with the Joneses.

Finally, a note of contradiction. It's been written that woods gathering caused great environmental concern. In the book *The Vegetation of the New Jersey Pine-Barrens*, originally printed in 1916, John W. Harshberger writes, "The income derived from the sale of greens for decoration, especially at Christmas time, and of wild flowers for bouquets, has been considerable to the people of the New Jersey pine forest. The collection of these materials has been so careless and wasteful in past years that the supply of some of

Judd Cawley and his black lab Teal on the Mullica River, Lower Bank, New Jersey. *Artist Kristan Barcalow.*

them is exhausted almost and all persons interested in the conservation of our vegetation and our natural resources should cry a halt." It's a concerning statement and paints an inverse picture to what an environmental hero would look like today. It is also contrary to the research this book is based on. Harshberger mentions in the same chapter of his book the "Cranberry Culture," "Huckleberry Picking" and "Drug Plants" that were collected and used medicinally for a span of 250 years. Odd that nothing is stated about any of these enterprises negatively affecting the environment, whereas the actions of the poor Pineys, or what he calls "the people of the New Jersey pine forest," were in need of scrutiny. Remember it was in this period when, in 1912, Dr. Goddard's book on the Kallikaks was printed and "Piney" became a derogatory word. It seems there was a natural bias toward the work the Pineys were doing. Certainly, we all can agree today that rules and regulations to protect overfishing are a good thing. Similarly, the late twentieth-century Pineycraft trade or dried floral industry would have benefited from government regulations too. Hindsight is always 20/20.

# The Piney Outlaws

A 1983 movie based on the book *The Outsiders* by S.E. Hinton has become a cult classic, with a famous cast including Patrick Swayze, Tom Cruise, C. Thomas Howell, Matt Dillon, Ralph Macchio, Rob Lowe and Emilio Estevez. The characters had brushes with the law, had colorful birth names and earned nicknames like Ponyboy Curtis, Dallas "Dally" Winston, Johnny Cade, Darrel "Darry" Curtis, Sodapop Curtis and Keith "Two-Bit" Matthews. They used colorful slang terms for more than just names of people; the "Cooler" was the town jail.

The Pineys from that same period had some crazy colorful nicknames, which to outsiders made it hard to figure out who was who. They also used slang terms for Pineycraft picking locations, as they often needed a name for others to understand where to meet up but there was no real name of those specific locations. This lexicon of slang was unique to them, similar to Hinton's novel.

The remaining Pineys in the 1980s knew of one another and heard the news about one another from John Richardson or one of the other buyers. They all sold their Pineycraft items to the highest bidders. They only recognized each other by their slang nicknames. Like a CliffsNotes version summary, somewhere buried in this comparison of the movie to real life is how there are two different worlds running parallel to each other, only being separated by the classification of Pineys versus non-Pineys.

See a small list below of real-life Piney nicknames (assembled with help from Judd Cawley):

| | | |
|---|---|---|
| Mud Duck | Tick | Skin Jim |
| Junior | Outlaw | Gordy |
| Gilly-Eyed Gang | Junie | Bond Baker |
| Cowboy | The Duke | Roy |
| JR (like *Dallas*) | Peany | Dirty Dave |
| Doll | Reds | Teddy Bear |
| One-Eyed Harry | Pumper Will | Little Johnny |
| Jack of Diamonds | Snuffy | Punk |
| Joe Boy | Big Sam | Turtle under the Bridge |
| Indian | Crazy Hazy | |

Following is a list of Piney names for favorite gathering and hunting sites and the items to be found there, again provided by Judd Cawley:

| Back Creek (San Fran Road) | cattails, muskrat trapping |
|---|---|
| Blackberry Creek | cattails, muskrat trapping |
| Bone Yard | hogbrush, sweethuck, birch |
| Bubbling Hill | hogbrush, sweethuck, deer hunting |
| Burnt Bridge | elkshorn, buttons |
| Colony | sweethuck, deer hunting |
| Crossroads | sweethuck |
| Curry Pond | birch, cats paws |
| Dead Man's Road | birch, deer hunting |
| Dultys | grapevine, brown burr, bell grass, bittersweet, fern center, birch, heather, horsemint |
| Forty Bucks | hogbrush, deer hunting, fox and coyote trapping |
| Gold Mine | elkshorn, buttons, orange buds |
| Goose Pond | deer, duck hunting |
| Green Fox Bridge | hogbrush |
| Gregory's | grapevine, birch, fern center |
| Muddy Road | hogbrush, deer hunting |
| Old Lady Haines (Bill Haines's wife's cabin) | birch, sweethuck, duck hunting |
| Paradise | hogbrush, pickerel fishing, deer hunting |
| Sandy Road | hogbrush, duck hunting |
| Sim Place | birch, laurel, cats paws |
| Three Bridges | birch, hogbrush |
| Three Mile Road | sea statice |

Here is a story describing one of the most famous tales told among Pineys and the funniest run-in with the law that a Piney from the above group had. It is almost like a scene out of *The Outsiders*.

*Judd Cawley says his buddy Freddy Erwine tells the story best, as he tells it with that Chatsworth accent we all had back in the day. The story goes, "One day Turtle (Donald Simcox) and a guy named John Babe went out drinking and driving throughout the Pines, as was a thing to do back then. Now Turtle earned his nickname due to the identical cartoonish tattoos on both his arms of a turtle. Well, John and Turtle started down in Chatsworth. They were raising hell with their pickup truck heading north on those back sandy roads and ran out of beer. So they went into Browns Mills, as that was the closest town.*

*After they got a case of one of America's cheapest beers—Old Milwaukee—they were heading back to the woods roads from whence they came and a cop pulled behind them. And when he flipped his flashing blue and red lights on the patrol car, they put the pedal to the floor and started to outrun the cops. They were out front for a little bit before the cops started to catch up to them. Seeing the cops were going to overtake them, they come to a bridge and Turtle pulls the car over in a hurry and he jumps out of the car and hides under the bridge. John Babe in the passenger seat, three sheets to the wind, is just sitting there when up walks the cop. The cop asks him, "Where's the driver, as I know you weren't by yourself in the car?" Mind you, John was so drunk he didn't even think to jump out of the car and run from the cops. In typical country bumpkin Chatsworth drawl John responds to the cop's question, "Turtle under the bridge." And the cop says, "There's all kinds of turtles under the bridge. Now where is your buddy at?" John repeated the phrase "Turtle under the bridge" and insisted that he was telling the cop where Turtle was. The cop repeated, angrily this time, "Yeah, there are turtles under the bridge. Now where the hell is your buddy?" The story ends with John taking a trip with the police to the Pemberton station and Turtle getting away and acquiring an extension to his nickname. From that day forward, forever to be known as Turtle under the Bridge by friends.*

Chapter 5

# Societal Safety Net Suffocates Piney Independence

Not all of the blame for the shifting winds on the Piney way of life can be attributed to the culture shift toward land preservation, or the culture of preservation. The Goddard and Kite factor ushered in the popular thought that those in the Pine Barrens area needed society's help. From the first publishing of the Goddard study in 1912, the "Independent and Free lifestyle" of the Pineys was threatened. They had been left to their own devices, which led them down a fiery spiral staircase directly to hell along with the most famous Piney, the Jersey Devil. (That statement was sarcasm, as we have illustrated up to this point that the typical Piney was a hardworking, interconnected member of his community, but it didn't stop politicians from using it for their own political gain, right, Mr. Fielder?)

While this new focus from outsiders led some Pineys to be institutionalized in the early 1900s in the Burlington County Colony for Feeble-Minded Boys at New Lisbon, which first opened in 1913 before transitioning to state control in 1916, it also led to state funding to assist the people in an area that was perceived as being severely impoverished. And is this an untrue belief? From the early days in the Pines, life was tough working at one of the iron furnaces or a glass factory. And later, after farming moved in, those who worked the farm did not consider themselves to be well off. Most families were one injury away from needing public support that could be received from a local church almshouse.

Across New Jersey, poor relief evolved from the sole responsibility of almshouses to public funding even though voluntary charitable organizations still served an important role in the lives of the indigent. Commissioner of the Department of Institutions and Agencies William J. Ellis states in his writings, titled *Public Welfare in New Jersey 1630–1944*, "1911 First modernization of Poor Relief law. Permitted aid to persons in temporary distress without sacrifice of civil rights inherent in Colonial poor law concepts." This acknowledged the need for temporary public assistance while being underemployed or not employed at all while the indigent continued to be able to vote. And later in the 1930s, major change occurred due to the change in public opinion. Before, it was local churches taking care of the needy and individual responsibility to fend for oneself that kept people from starving and needing or wanting the government to assist.

Then in 1933, President Franklin Delano Roosevelt took office with the New Deal with public works projects affecting the working poor. A lot of New Jersey parks today still are evidence of the hands of the many volunteers in the Civilian Conservation Corps (CCC), which was a six-month assignment to put the youth of America to work. In a video recording of a radio announcement in March 1933, FDR states, "Men of the Civilian Conservation Corps, in speaking to you tonight I am thinking of you as a visible token of encouragement to the whole country. Through you, the nation will graduate a fine group of strong young men, clean living, trained to self-discipline and above all willing and proud to work for the joy of working. That, my friends, must be the new spirit of the American future. And you are the vanguard of that new spirit." The work of a workforce made up of all males ages eighteen to twenty-five helped lift some Pineys out of poverty, and their work benefited Pinelands parks like Bass River State Forest in Tuckerton, Belleplain State Forest in Woodbine, Brendan T. Byrne State Forest in New Lisbon and Penn State Forest in New Gretna. But it also took the Piney out of the woods, lessening the chances they would return to their traditional roots.

In the 1960s, both at the federal and state level, there was an expansion of the welfare system. At the federal level, Charles Murray wrote in his monumental book *Losing Ground: American Social Policy, 1950–1980*, "On top of all these efforts was a huge expansion in the transfer of money and in-kind support. The principal components of the cash increases were expansions in public assistance Aid to Families with Dependent Children (AFDC), Social Security and its associated programs, Unemployment Insurance, and general welfare assistance in the form of 'Supplemental Security Income.' The eligibility rules for the AFDC were liberalized first through the 1962 Social Security Amendments." And later, the government work continued to assist the poor in the period of 1964 to 1967. Murray writes, "The principal components of the in-kind transfers were Medicaid (for low-income persons), Medicare (for Social Security beneficiaries), Food Stamps, and housing programs." The Pineys of that generation who never worked a forty-hour workweek instantly became eligible for state assistance or, as it was called then, relief. Many families who had worked for generations collecting pinecones or were hired on at a blueberry farm to prune rows of blueberry bushes by hand were sometimes paid under-the-table wages. There were no receipts kept in "Pineyville." The conventional way of determining if people needed public assistance was to look at earned wages, or lack thereof. Instantly, if a Piney was approached by a relief service agent, he or she would qualify for assistance. And besides the unreported income, the dried floral business wasn't as lucrative for Pineys as it was for the proprietors of said goods.

It's unknown how many Pineys in South Jersey became dependents of the state in the 1960s and 1970s. There had to be a huge personal struggle with those who became dependent on government assistance or welfare to transition to full-time employment. For one thing, a Piney's "woods degree" became a handicap toward his integration into the waged working class. If you recall when we interviewed a neighboring farmer to the Richardsons, he stated that "they were independent, which learned a trade that was passed on by generation to generation." Being a Piney was like being part of a social institution of the Pine Barrens or in a tribe. It illustrated that Pineys' tacit knowledge was highly coveted in the family and passed down in a hands-on fashion, continuing the generational tradition of collecting items from the land. There was no formal schooling cheerleader in the family pushing children to go to school, let alone to pursue advanced academic degrees in colleges. So children of Pineys were less than enthusiastic about going to school in the first place, and most jobs in the industrial commonwealth were seeking qualified candidates with a minimum of a high school diploma.

Secondly, among those interviewed in preparation for this writing, there was a common theme of alcohol use and abuse in Pineys. This is interconnected with the dependency on relief or welfare or other forms of government assistance like food stamps. One woman interviewed said, "Nothing easy about living off the land. Pineys aren't ignorant, and the ones that went out and had a drink were probably unwinding at the end of a hard day." Adding to her point that it was hard living, by being your own boss you had to be self-disciplined, ever pushing to pick or collect enough of the Pineycraft item of the day to support yourself and your family, as there were no personal sick or vacation days to be used. Normal holidays like Fourth of July were worked as well.

And at the end of a long day, some unwound with spirits. Others relieved stress in other, more healthful ways, but alcoholism is a disease that is delivered in the form of the devil in a bottle. Now if you were lucky enough to be a Piney and get government assistance, it became increasingly harder to talk yourself into going out in the humid summer air to cut cattails instead of having leisure time accompanied by a drink or two using the money from your relief check. This is from where the term "Friday Night Pineys" was derived to describe those Pineys—not all but a small number—who only worked a few days a week in the woods, making enough to buy a case of beer and thereby meeting their only want. So the lack of proper schooling and alcohol dependency were factors in preventing some Pineys from making that transition from traditional woods work to a full-time, forty-hour workweek. But for most, the transition occurred more rapidly than most would have wanted.

If you Google *homogeneous*, your result is "of the same kind; alike." Cultural homogeny's greatest driver in the history of developed nations has been the need for currency to meet basic human needs. The necessity for Pineys to adapt to a new lifestyle, albeit forced upon them, that accompanies the forty-hour industrial workweek shaped them into the cookie-cutter mold of other New Jerseyans moving to the South Jersey area in the Pines seeking the same solitude and beauty the Pineys already enjoyed. In 1982, an epic foreshadowing of things to come for the Pineys occurred in a televised WPIX interview at the New Jersey Folk Festival. Dr. Angus Gillespie made this profound statement: "One of the things that makes Pine Barrens a special and interesting place is the people who lived there had deliberately dropped out of the mainstream. To the extinct that Pineys have joined the rest of us through media such as television, they will be with every passing year I fear less distinctive, less unusual. We are moving in the direction of a homogenous culture." The doctor hit the nail on the head with that little bit of foreshadowing.

Whether they took work with the burgeoning cranberry and blueberry industries or took up a trade, this started the end of the traditional Piney and marched the Piney tribe toward the homogeneous culture society wanted them to join.

Now mind you, we're talking about a certain type of Piney, and each of us knows there are different types of people in life and there are different types of Pineys (as we will explain later in this book). Let's just say for now the "Woods Piney" or "Reluctant Piney" could have been the title of this book, as the majority of this book is describing that type of Piney who begrudgingly joined New Jersey's homogeneous society. But it wasn't just the Woods Piney who conformed; the other types of Pineys did as well, in their own due time.

## DEVELOPMENTS AFFECTING THE PEOPLE OF THE NEW JERSEY PINE BARRENS AREA

1891–2017: Willis Jefferson Buzby purchases Chatsworth General Store. It had many other owners after Buzby, but author R. Marilyn Schmidt, who passed away in 2019, is credited with saving and reopening the store from 1998 to 2017.

1905: Bass River State Forest, one of the state's first state forests, is acquired.

1912: H.H. Goddard publishes *The Kallikak Family: A Study in the Heredity of Feeble Mindedness*.

1913, June 28: Governor James Fielder calls out Pineys for being New Jersey degenerates after Elizabeth Kite's research paper is published.

1913: The 1911 New Jersey Sterilization Law is passed. It is the first U.S. law to ever be declared unconstitutional.

1914, July 28–1918, November 11: World War I. The United States enters in 1917.

1916: Botanist Frederick Coville and Elizabeth White sell the first commercial crop of blueberries out of Whitesbog, New Jersey.

1917: Fort Dix is established as a military training base.

1919: The Eighteenth Amendment is passed prohibiting the sale of alcohol.

1924: Immigration Restriction Act (ban on eastern European immigrants— Russians, Italians, Hungarians and Jews) is passed.

1926: The State of New Jersey establishes the first forest tree nursery in Jackson Township.

1929: The stock market crash occurs and the Great Depression begins (October 1929–1939).

1930: Ocean Spray is founded by Marcus Urann, John Makepeace and Elizabeth Lee. The first product is Jellied Cranberry Sauce.

1932: John Richardson purchases the floral business from his mother. John takes orders, and his mother, Hanna, and brother, Lester, help fulfill them.

1933: The Twenty-First Amendment is passed, repealing the Eighteenth. New Jersey is the fifth state to approve it, on June 1, 1933, and enough states approve it for ratification on December 5, 1933.

1933: The Civilian Conservation Corps (CCC) is established and continues through the early 1940s.

1937: The Pic-A-Lilli Inn is renamed for daughter Lillian of Thomas Synder, who ran a luncheonette at the site since 1927.

1939, September 1–1945, September 2: World War II. The United States enters in 1941.

1945: John Richardson purchases Mount Holly Fairgrounds.

1947, June 6: *Mount Holly Herald* prints "Gamblers Jittery as Police Dragnet Closes; 10 Nabbed."

1950s: American automobile culture emerges.

1951: The New Jersey Turnpike opens.

1954: Forest fires rage in Chatsworth.

1955: The stock market soars, passing earlier 1929 high.

1955: Richardson sells Mount Holly Fairgrounds, which becomes a shopping plaza.

1955: The State of New Jersey purchases 100,000-acre Wharton Tract as a state forest.

1955–58: John Richardson pays $75,000 for a farm and 250 acres of Forest P. Harker. He builds horse stalls and a racetrack for training harness racehorses and remodels the existing farmhouse there on Jobstown-Jacksonville Road.

1956: Abner and "Babe" Nixon open Nixon's General Store and Deli. Grandson Jack and Nancy McGinnis run it for thirty-five years. It was under new owners as of June 2018.

1960: John Richardson sells rancher on Monmouth Road with twenty-four acres and rents a Jobstown house on the corner.

1961–75: Vietnam War era.

1962–63: The dried floral business wanes from competition with plastic(s), flowers and birch trees.

1963: One of the largest Pinelands wildfires burns nearly 190,000 acres.

1965: Richardsons move to 294 Sykesville Road in Chesterfield, New Jersey; business is starting to rebound.

1965: A policeman is caught in the Pine Barrens after setting a total of sixty-nine forest fires.

1967: John McPhee's *The Pine Barrens* is published, introducing people to the image of a Piney in Bill Wasiowich.

1967: The dried floral business has an uptick as the desire for natural items is trending.

1971: Micks Canoe and Kayak Rental original owners were brothers George and Howard Mick. For the last eighteen years, it was owned and operated by Howard Chew and Tom Azzara at 3107 Route 563 in Chatsworth.

1973–74: Johnny Richardson moves to 396 Sykesville Road, Wrightstown.

1975: Lucille's Luncheonette opens in Warren Grove, New Jersey, by proprietor Lucille Bates Wickward.

1977–78: The Richardsons move to 400 Sykesville Road, Wrightstown.

1978: Congress establishes Pinelands National Reserve, 1.1 million acres (53 percent permanently protected).

1979: Pinelands Commission creates and enacts Pinelands Protect Act (PPA).

1979: First appearance in print of the slogan "Piney Power" on the front door of Johnny Brooms's cement-block restaurant and pool hall on Main Street in Chatsworth.

1981: Pinelands Comprehensive Management Plan (CMP) is enacted.

1983: The Chatsworth Cranberry Festival is established.

1989–90: The dried floral business's heyday ends; increased imports and introduced silk flowers are to blame.

1989: Robyn Bednar opens Hot Diggidy Dog on 3970 Main Street, Chatsworth.

1993: Pine Barrens Jamboree is established.

1994, December: John Richardson passes away. The once thriving dried floral industry of New Jersey dies with him.

2003: Miller's Cranberry Hot Sauce is created by Robin Miller in Indian Mills, Shamong Township.

2005: March Lines on the Pines festival is founded by Linda Stanton.

Chapter 6

# *Piney Bumper Stickers*

It isn't all that important to tell the history of the Piney bumper sticker to understand what seeing people have them on their vehicles means to Pineys. The bumper sticker with various renditions of Piney pride sayings marks a cultural break from the term "Piney" being a negative to a positive. The famous locales in the Pines that became tourist attractions were capitalized on similar to the novelty and appeal to Americans of the *Beverly Hillbillies* TV show in the 1960s and 1970s. Just prior, the New Jersey Turnpike opened in 1951 and fueled the exploration and popularization of faraway places in the Pines like Buzby's General Store in Chatsworth, Lucille's Diner in Warren Grove and Nixon's General Store & Deli in Tabernacle.

In the early 1980s, a local anonymous South Jersey farmer was riding along in a pickup truck on a road in Burlington County with friend Ernie Richardson. Ernie and his brothers Lester and John were known to have done Piney work collecting Pineycraft items, starting in the 1920s. Ernie loved trapping as much as he did collecting sphagnum moss or the like in the Pines. Heading nowhere specific, the two observed another pickup truck in front of them that was turning to go toward the town of Wrightstown and had a "Proud to Be a Piney" bumper sticker on it. Ernie said, "Look at that guy. He's got a bumper sticker that says he's proud to be a Piney. Proud to be a Piney—that had to be a joke." In general, the term Piney had always been used in a negative way to Ernest, and by no means did the Pineys own the term, as it was taken away from them by making it a bad word in the early 1900s. To Ernie, the word Piney would always be a derogatory term.

Cathy Antener with her "Piney Power" bumper sticker news clipping. *From the* SandPaper, *March 14, 2007.*

Prior to that incident with Ernie Richardson, there was a Piney Power bumper sticker craze in the late 1970s that marked a new way for a generation of Pineys to take back the term. It became popular not just with insiders but outsiders of the Pine Barrens too. The meaning of the original phrase got lost when outsiders adopted it, but it originally was meant to unite the local community and show defiance to the state and federal government's overreach. In the Pines, you found yourself with little modern conveniences, which made you resourceful and independent. The question was never, "Who is going to help me?" but more of a shared statement: "When we gonna get this done?" In the '70s, it was the locals' way of pushing back on the new directive telling them what they could and could not do with their land in the newly established Pinelands National Reserve.

The backstory of who was the first person to put to print the various Piney slogans was undiscoverable during the research of this book. A Facebook commentator stated, "I remember seeing the Piney Power ones (from Green Bank Inn), pretty much my whole life so that would be back into the mid-70s. The proud to be Piney ones didn't come about until the early 90s and they used to sell them at Pine Bay Liquors on 539." An anonymous person interviewed suggested that Piney Power came about in the late 1960s and or early 1970s. At the same time, there was a popular political slogan, Black Power, in the 1960s and 1970s among the African American community. But in an interview with Alice Cawley, she remembered, "The Piney Power name was used when I was a kid, and I heard it firsthand from my dad, Walt Horton, and his three brothers (Jerry, Buck and Clarance), who bootlegged in the Chatsworth area in the 1930s, and they loved telling stories of the old days, referencing the Piney Power slogan and bootlegging in the same breath."

In an April 5, 1979 article in the *New York Times* titled "Ban on Construction Divides Jersey Pine Barrens," Donald Janson wrote, "The red and white 'piney power' slogans, plastered on Johnny Brooms's front door and seven-stool counter mean that 'pineys' who have been here for generations want to be as free as anyone outside the infertile Barrens to decide whether to keep their land as is, put a new house on it, try to cultivate it, or sell it for housing projects." The *New York Times* sent a reporter in April to write about the politically charged atmosphere in the Pine Barrens just two months after Governor Brendan Byrne signed Executive Order 71, which basically halted all new development in the Pinelands for eighteen months, on February 8, 1979. This was viewed as a major overstep by the governor. South Jersey had the public spotlight placed on it by the 1967 publishing of John McPhee's book *The Pine Barrens* and the establishment in 1978 of the Pinelands National Reserve. The local response to that attention was to unite behind the old slogan "Piney Power."

In the 1987 book *Pinelands Folklife*, written by Rita Moonsammy, David S. Cohen and Lorraine E. Williams, there is a photo on page one of Vincentown resident and second-generation farmworker Orlando Torres wearing a baseball cap with the words "Piney Power" boldly printed on it. During a recent phone interview with PineyPower.com website owner and Barnegat resident Cathy Antener, she said, "I remember seeing a sign off of the Green Bank Inn in Washington Township that said 'Piney Power' in the '80s." She had created a website on Geocities in 1996 to collect information about the Pine Barrens. And when she was approached to move the hosting of the website to a server and rename her site, registering it as PineyPower.com in 1998, that was that. Cathy says in the early years there were people coming up to her at events in the Pines like the Pine Barrens Jamboree held in Waretown, which she attended to promote her website, asking her for Piney Power bumper stickers and T-shirts.

So the public's attitude toward that bumper sticker was either passive or aggressively in favor of it.

But there is a lot to overcome in stereotypes associated with the Pines New Jersey already has its own bad reputation for having one of the highest densities of people in the United States and having miles of highways and interstates. Outsiders only see New Jersey as a road in between two of the East Coast's largest cities, New York City and Philadelphia. South Jersey Pinelands has that same reputation to some of its own residents. If you explore the Pine Barrens, you'll come to see that once you get off that asphalt highway and get on a dirt road, that misconception melts away into pure bliss. All Pineys understand this. More and more outsiders have come to learn of the unique areas of the Pines from social media outlets like Facebook and Instagram and annually visit. Still many people in the Tristate area only hear of the Pines from someone else, never visiting and seeing the beauty with their own eyes.

Take, for instance, the MTV television sensations of *Jersey Shore*. MTV personality Jenni "JWoww" Farley was one of those who never visited the Pinelands but formulated her opinion of the Pines from a less than flattering description given to her by New Jersey native costar and MTV celebrity Deena Cortese. In an episode of the popular MTV reality show *Jersey Shore*, the women went camping, and Deena explained to JWoww the Pineys and the Jersey Devil. In an interview for the *Jersey Shore Massacre* movie printed in the *Daily Record* newspaper on August 24, 2014, JWoww stated, "Doing this movie reminded so much of when Deena had to explain the Pineys to me. It's kind of like the backwoods of the Jersey Shore where the crazy people live. If there's any place to have a serial killer, it would be the Pineys."

But hey, newspapers sometimes can get the facts wrong, right, Mrs. Kite? The online news source Phillymag.com wrote an article on February 12, 2016, titled "13 Things You Might Not Know about the Pine Barrens," and did thorough fact-checking, with a quote from Kite acknowledging that her report had tarnished and misused the term "Piney." Kite said, "Nothing would give me greater pleasure than to correct the idea that has unfortunately been given by the newspapers regarding the pines….I think it is a most terrible calamity that the newspapers publicly took the term and gave it the degenerate sting." Insert story of Ernie seeing a "Proud to Be a Piney" bumper sticker for the first time and still being embarrassed by the term in the late 1980s. Ernie laughed at the bumper sticker, knowing from his past experience that many looked down on people who were labeled Pineys. In hindsight, we can say Ernie was wrong to laugh at that sticker, and he himself should have had one on his truck. Loving where you come from, which helps make up who you are, doesn't make you any less of a human being than anyone else. Being honest with yourself, taking the good experiences and not so good and forging ahead in life to be happy, is something we all should hope for in our own lives. That degenerate sting still lingers, but with continued efforts to take it back in the form of two bumper stickers—"Proud to Be a Piney" and "Piney Power"—we have moved closer to the public forgetting the old negative stereotype associated with the term and replacing it with a more powerful and positive meaning in the twenty-first century.

Chapter 7

# Times a Changin'

The Reluctant Piney or the true Woods Piney way of life is all but dead. We could not preserve their way of life when the environmental movement has been so successful in protecting the Pine Barrens through the oversight of the Pinelands Commission, using the Comprehensive Management Plan as their guiding light. Along with the cultural dependency that ended the Reluctant Piney's way of life by living off the land, we have, for better or worse (depending on who you are), a preservation culture. In Jonathan Berger's book *Water, Earth, and Fire*, he spells out the issue: "Most planning difficulties occur in the attempts to analyze the human parts of systems; it is easier for scientists to describe the nonhuman environment than the people and cultures that exist in a region." In other words, most planners have trouble including humans in ecological planning. He sat down and wrote this book in 1985 to establish a planning tool that forewarned the coming issues the Pinelands Commission would run into. He clearly foresaw the challenges for Pineys as land preservation became the only means to protect and manage the new national reserve in Southern New Jersey.

He goes on to say:

*What is so valuable about the old ways, the seasonal activities, and family and community ties? Surely, intrinsic interest is part of the value—the old way of doing things, crafts, folktales, and work. More important is that seasonal life-styles reflect strong and mutually advantageous balances among people and their resources. These balances evolve over time and mediate changes in the supply of food, water, shelter, and living space as human demand rises or falls. They have to do with subsistence, with survival without dependence on highly technological, capital-intensive processes. But the survival must be seen in human terms. People along the coast, indeed throughout the Pine Barrens, adapted themselves to live not only with their resources, but interdependently. Suburbanization and industrialization tend to break apart carefully constructed ways of doing things, of getting along. Once broken, the old ways are hard to piece together, and a whole series of adaptations fall apart.*

An elder in the Pine Barrens community gave a great interpretation of the new laws and why Pineys could not cut Pineycraft items on state land like they used to. In a conversation with the elder, this author recited a story of when Patrick Lewis's truck was impounded in the mid-1980s by the State Forest Service in Weymouth, New Jersey, for Lewis's illegal cutting of birch whips. The wise elder responded:

*More than there ever was they keep acquiring more ground. But naturally, it doesn't matter if you're picking up pebbles off the freaking ground. They're the people's pebbles. If you're gathering pinecones, they're the people's pebbles. I paid taxes to help buy that land. So it's everybody's land, and you can't be in there enriching yourself. It makes common sense. Off any natural resource, whether it's pinecones or dog fleas. There was a story circulating about cutting laurel and it being illegal anywhere in the state, but that was just a rumor. If I own a farm, I could cut laurel on my property. When it grows in a state forest, of course, there's a law because it doesn't belong to you. You can't get permission, or mostly you can't cut it. They took taxpayer dollars to purchase and preserve that land.*

So Pineys either have to move on or adapt, as the times they are a changin', like Bob Dylan sings.

Another Piney, Bill Wasiowich, tells of suffering the same fate as Patrick Lewis back in the late 1980s and early 1990s, only he was cutting sweethuck at what was then Lebanon State Forest (now Brendan T. Byrne), where his load was seized and he was ticketed the standard fifty-dollar fee. As Bill himself stated in 2020 during an interview at his place:

*You can't do it. You got to get written permission from the owner of that property to work out there. All you gotta do is read the state signs they put up. I don't know whether they give permits out anymore or not. And far as that goes, I don't know of anybody cutting anything out of these woods anymore. Anybody can go out there and get a little bit of stuff like you say, but you couldn't work in a professional way. That's what put me out of business. They won't let you pick pinecones out there. You can't cut the hogbrush or sweethuck.*

Again we can hear the frustration during the interviewing of those last-of-their-kind Pineys who were still trying to make a dollar or two out in the woods. When Bill was told "those were the days, huh?" he replied, "You can't turn the clock back. You gotta adapt to the kinda world you're living in." It sure does seem like good old country advice.

It seems no one writes about the dirt poor and uneducated people of the Pines other than the famous girl who was used as a prop to further a bigoted theory that feeblemindedness was hereditary. You just never hear about them. Sure, someone like the bigger-than-life character of John Richardson, who we've yet to introduce to the reader in this book, should have had a book or two written about him by now. I wonder why. Was there a natural bias because of the Piney characterization at the highest state level in the governor's office? Like I said, you'd never hear a story about the Cawleys, who lived like country bumpkins, but their contributions to the cultural and moral fabric of the Piney are felt today. Their voices and their stories need to be told. And they're just one family I interviewed.

You can see that sense of pride today if you sit down at Lucille's diner in Warren Grove and ask a local if they knew any Pineys. They'd reminisce about the old-time Pineys, and in that action you'd hear a sense of pride

Song written in 1979 by Lillian M. Lopez titled "Proud to Be a Piney." *Courtesy of Pinelands Cultural Society.*

from them just knowing a Piney or claiming to be a Piney themselves. Those Pineys who worked the woods are our connection to the generations before them who toiled in the paper mills, sawmills, glass factories and bog iron furnaces. And like those industries, the dried floral industry has faded into memories past.

As they say, times are a changin', and maybe it's time to let the world know we are proud of our Piney heritage and to give ourselves the gift of accepting our own heritage for what it is—a great example of the American pioneer spirit. Even the Richardsons struggled with the term "Piney." Their patriarch was listed in the 1930 census not as a sphagnum moss collector but as a proprietor. That family branch never claimed to be Pineys. You see today in their offspring a sense of pride from their part in the history of the Piney, and they claim the title of Piney for themselves today. The stigma of being labeled a moron and that nasty term being used as a synonym for Piney had a whole generation refusing their heritage— the good and the bad. As you read these words with the newly gained knowledge of their struggles for acceptance and for a good country living, you and I are righting that past wrong.

Thank the Piney gods that other types of Pineys today have transitioned and adapted to the fire of the times in the Pines and a latitude of these Pineys are living, breathing and thriving just as unique as the Pinelands that they inhabit. I started out by thinking the old Pineys were impoverished using today's standards, but that lens doesn't take into account their freedoms: freedom to one day be picking pinecones and the next be hunting deer along the rye fields of Warren Grove and the freedom to not be tied to another man's schedule but to be in tune with Mother Nature's schedule. That, to many, is pure nirvana.

As of this writing, there is a whole counterculture movement of sorts that continues to grow and is in agreement with how Pineys of yesterday lived, with no modern conveniences or need of electricity in their homes. As stated earlier, many Pineys lived deep in the woods and were hermit-like but also deeply connected to their surroundings. You can't live in the middle of what we know today as Wharton State Forest and expect to run a television, as there is no electricity to support it. As recently as 2006, Wikipedia reports, "On 13 April 2006, *USA Today* reported that there were 'some 180,000 families living off-grid, a figure that has jumped 33% a year for a decade,' and cited Richard Perez, publisher of *Home Power* magazine as the source." Many people, in trying to reduce their personal carbon footprints, are turning to reducing their families' dependence on fossil fuels. The Pineys of old would be proud of these folks seeking solace in the wilderness where it still exists, not only by eliminating the need for electricity but also becoming knowledgeable about foraging natural foods from the woods. It's truly an honorable thing to engage in activities such as living off the grid to meet one's bare essentials while maintaining that connection to nature.

In chapter 9, I go into identifying the main types or groups of Pineys. The reader may identify with more than one type of Piney but, when put to it, be resolved enough to choose which one or two best describes you. I listed these out as told to me by a wise old Piney woman named Sarah Lewis. There was no malfeasance in the process, more of an avoidance of war between the folks who like to declare an Us versus Them mentality. Webster defines parochialism as "the quality or state of being parochial; especially: selfish pettiness or narrowness (as of interests, opinions, or views)." But let's not lose our cultural identity by being so rigid with the definition of what a Piney was or is, and let's embrace who we've become.

Now, lest we forget what the Medford woman said in the book *Pinelands Folklife Project: One Space, Many Places*, her hard definition of a Piney was the Woods Piney or the Reluctant Piney used interchangeably, and it did not include "lumberers, trappers, farmers, or recently arrived ethnic groups." There will be hardliners in the Pine Barrens community who, through personal experience, are the real McCoy. And there are some in the community who have assumed the persona of what they think is a Piney for personal gain. Those charlatans should be called out for what they are: fakes and liars. We can love something and be part of it but need not lie about it and turn toward cultural appropriation. It's odd today to see some folks making money off the assumed Piney life when in fact they'd be reluctant to live that life, as poor as it was at times. And hard work—that's a phrase Pineys use a lot.

Please take a gander at these suggestions with an open heart and tell us we ain't wrong! Sometimes when you're picking pinecones and mostly staring down into your bucket of brown and green cones, you take a few steps forward and wind up on a hillock, and when you look up from your narrow view you get awestruck by the forest of pygmy pines before you. Take a moment and visualize yourself at the top of the fire tower on Apple Pie Hill gazing out at the waves of green. We're looking for folks to take that larger view of what a Piney is today and put an end to the debate about who can wear the title of "Piney."

But first, who was at the center, at the very beginning, of the traditional pinecone-picking Woods Piney or the Reluctant Piney? We mentioned his surname, Richardson, in earlier chapters. The following chapter tells the life history of one man whose lifeblood is as amber as the sap that oozes from the pine trees of the Pinelands. He lived his life by his rules, and like the fire that opened up the serotinous pinecones of the plains, his life was propelled forward by the fire of failure to the rebirth of the phoenix, finally soaring once he realized his life's work was with the Pineys. And if you have one of those Pineys, Reluctant or Woods Pineys, somewhere in your family tree, you should be darn proud of it!

Chapter 8

# Once Upon a Time

## JOHN RICHARDSON'S 101 ITEMS

An interconnected supply chain of wholesale dried floral supplies that were used in New York City and Philadelphia storefront displays up until 1994 may have originated from a farmstead located at 400 Sykesville Road in Wrightstown, New Jersey. The Pineys called the proprietor John Richardson or ole' man Jack.

Our exclusive story starts and ends with one of the greatest old-time entrepreneurial families of the day. The Richardson family helped foster and sustain the Piney way of life for hundreds of Piney families across a span of seventy-plus years. The entrepreneurial spirit of the eldest son, John Richardson, who went on to run the family business, would expand the diversity of dried floral offerings to the hungry floral markets in the Northeast and provide self-employment to the independent and free-spirited Pineys of South Jersey. From the start of the dried floral business in Mount Holly, New Jersey, in 1920 to the final days of John Richardson in 1994, a Piney who knew where to go picking for the woods item of the day never went hungry, as he had a way to make a buck. Until the very end in 1994, on a hilltop in Wrightstown, New Jersey, behind a white picket fence, one of the most important brokers of various naturally grown items found in the wilds of the Pines of New Jersey was housed. Reluctant Pineys' lifeblood and John Richardson's were intertwined.

As told to us by his son, John M. Richardson—or, as he goes by today, Johnny—our story begins in the 1920s on a busy Pine Street at house number 25 in Mount Holly, New Jersey. The retelling of the story is that Mrs. Hanna

Richardson Wholesale Dry Florist, 400 Sykesville Road, Wrightstown, New Jersey. *Artist Kristan Barcalow.*

(Horner) Richardson had been approached by some city folk who asked if she could get them some pin oak branches, which were bursting with oranges and would serve as typical fall foliage decorations for a Philadelphia store display. She filled that order with the help of her children, and then another ask came for handmade laurel ropes or swags to be used for decorating in the Christmas season.

Hanna came from the Pine Barrens. She had a sister named Flo. John Richardson's daughter Pamela Holmes recalls being told that half of her grandmother's family, the Horners, stayed Piney and the other half became "citified." She remembers that at her grandmother's home on Pine Street, they popped pinecones over the center of the heater grate. The heat would open the pinecones, which had been picked when they were closed.

Having to feed so many mouths, the need for the business was born. Hanna (Horner) Richardson (1879–1967) and husband Joseph Richardson (1872–1950), an Irishman, had three sons and a daughter: Madeline (1900–1953); John (1902–1994); Ernest (1908–1984), nicknamed Ernie;

the COMPANY PINEY

the CONWAY TWITTY PINEY

the EDUCATED PINEY

the FIREFIGHTER PINEY

the HUNTER PINEY

the OUT of TOWN PINEY

the *PATRIOTIC PINEY*

the *SAMMY da CLAMMY PINEY*

the *WOODS PINEY*

the *TREEHUGGER PINEY*

*Top*: *From left to right*:
Pineys Hazelton
Dilks, Joseph Lewis
and Judd Cawley
showing tools of
the trade. *Author's
collection.*

*Bottom*: On
Central Railroad
in Manchester
Township, New
Jersey, sits an empty
chair representing
the people of the
Pines who have
gone before us.
*Author's collection.*

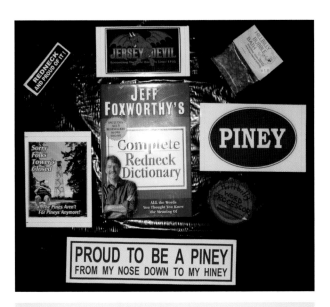

*Top*: People have been marginalized in various U.S. locations for generations. *Author's collection.*

*Bottom*: Sand road crossing the plains off Route 539. It is known as the pygmy forest of the New Jersey Pine Barrens. *Author's collection.*

Atlantic white cedar planters, a Pineycraft item from yesterday. *Author's collection.*

Wrapped, locally sourced grapevine wreaths, another Pineycraft. *Author's collection.*

Birch swan, original design by Judd Cawley. *Author's collection.*

Joseph Lewis demonstrating how to cut cattails. *Author's collection.*

*Left:* In the upper left-hand corner sits A.J. Cawley, along with Uncle Judd Cawley, *bottom center*, pulling fern centers. *Author's collection.*

*Below*: A peach basket of pinecones pulled while wearing heavy gloves to prevent injury. *Author's collection.*

Pinecones were sold closed to wholesale dried floral buyers, who had to open the cones prior to selling to the retail market. *Author's collection.*

Sweethuck or sugarhuck heart design, another Pineycraft. *Author's collection.*

*Above*: Author William Lewis standing near a display of thirty-plus Pineycraft items. *Author's collection.*

*Left*: Atlantic white cedar swamp. *Author's collection.*

*Right*: Birch whips were cut and sold to the dried floral market by the thousands. *Author's collection.*

*Below*: The Piney name of this bog plant species is elkshorn; the binomial is *Lophiola aurea*. *Author's collection.*

*Above*: The Piney name is snakeweed, more commonly called moth mullein. *Author's collection.*

*Left*: Cranberry bog pumphouse at Whitesbog Village, Browns Mills, New Jersey. *Author's collection.*

*Above*: Old cranberry sluice gate at Jumping Brook Preserve, New Egypt, New Jersey. *Author's collection.*

*Left*: Turkey beard (*Xerophyllum asphodeloides*), a Pineycraft item. *Author's collection.*

Judd Cawley with a bale of penny cress, sold by the pound in the dried floral industry heyday ending in the 1990s. *Dennis McDonald*.

Joseph Lewis pulling penny cress and bunching it, making it easy to be hung upside down and dried for the retail dried floral industry. *Dennis McDonald*.

Richardson family portrait on postcard. *Right to left*: Hanna, Lester, John, Madeline and Ernest. *Richardson family collection.*

and Lester (1911–1966), nicknamed Lec. Fast-forward in time—John had a son named Johnny and daughter named Pam, Ernie never had children and Lec had a total of six children: twin boys Dale and Gary, twin girls Patricia and a stillborn baby girl and a daughter Carole and a son named Ronnie.

In the Richardsons' lifetime, America experienced the 1929 stock market crash and the Great Depression of 1929–39. It was during this period that the Richardson family expanded the seasonal Christmas dried floral business offering. Miles and miles of laurel rope were gathered, and Mrs. Richardson usually used her three sons to fill the different contracts. Whether it was for a Christmas wreath made out of grapevine or a load of pinecones picked from the plains of South Jersey, she was able to meet the demand and supplement her family's income. Even during the Depression, city dealers still came to Mrs. Richardson seeking to have her fill orders for the city floral markets, which some say existed as early as the 1870s. The general population may have been unemployed, but those well-to-do still were buying flower arrangements even in the tough economic times.

To really understand the business that helped Pineys live an independent and free lifestyle, one needs to have an appreciation for the dried floral industry in America, especially in the Northeast. The ebb and flow of currency between wholesalers and self-employed individuals to the wholesalers and retailers had its cyclical extreme highs and natural lows. The Richardsons suffered many setbacks along the way, but they survived in a business built on dried flowers. We know that the Great Depression tightened Americans' belts, with families stretching an earned dollar to the point it was ripped apart beyond recognition. But during this period, there were winners and losers and super poor and super rich families. Both established floral markets in the Northeast—Philadelphia Market on JFK Boulevard and New York City at Seventh Avenue and Broadway—continued business as usual. This sustained demand helped the Richardsons' business keep its head above water.

In 1932, eldest son John, being all of thirty, took over the business, which was still located at 25 Pine Street in Mount Holly, by purchasing it from his mother. His mother and brothers would continue to help him fulfill special orders of items for the market. John, a savvy businessman, would go on to run the family business until the day he died in December 1994—a span of sixty-two years. Ask people who knew John to describe him in one word, and 99 percent of the time people would say *lucky*. As luck would have it, he got one of those once-in-a-lifetime opportunities in 1933 from a business at Thirteenth and Callowhill Street in Philadelphia. R&B Floral Design (Rice and Beiersdorfer) contracted with him to gather a plant that grew in the salt meadows along the Jersey seashore.

They were in a retail business where John was a wholesaler. Seizing upon this lucky opportunity and knowing that it could lead to landing a large partner in the dried floral industry, John took his two brothers Ernie and Lec with the largest truck they owned, which was nothing more than a beat-up International that had bad brakes. Somehow, they successfully cut and loaded the truck to the max with a bed of purply sea statice and, again, with some of John's luck were able to make it from Mount Holly to Philadelphia, crossing the Delaware River over the Ben Franklin Bridge with an overloaded truck having no brakes. Can you imagine the scene of it— three young, sweaty and dirty brothers squeezed into a small cab of an old 1930s International stake truck with eldest brother John driving, Lec riding shotgun with a Lucky Strike cigarette hanging out of his mouth and poor Ernie squished in the middle?

They safely brought the delivery to R&B Floral Designs on Callowhill Street. The owners were ecstatic with the delivery and would help John's expansion and ultimate dominance in the Philadelphia floral market. Afterward, John had a sign made up for the side of the truck that read, "Once Upon A Time—John Richardson 101 Items." Future orders included sea statice, which they painted in-house; cattails; pinecones; birch poles and twigs; grasses; and many other items that John would suggest to flower retailers. Companies like R&B Floral Designs brought the Piney pickings to the big cities, filling many noteworthy storefronts not just in the big cities of the Northeast like New York City and Philadelphia but nationwide.

Even at a young age, Jack (John's nickname) had a natural way with people. One of the common threads that tie all the different types of Pineys together is that, collectively, they were known to have extreme trust issues, especially with outsiders. But it was said that Jack could talk a lawman out of enforcing a law after a few hours of small talk. He knew the Pine Barrens

| | |
|---|---|
| **Name:** | John Richardson |
| **Respondent:** | Yes |
| **Age:** | 39 |
| **Estimated birth year:** | abt 1901 |
| **Gender:** | Male |
| **Race:** | White |
| **Birthplace:** | New Jersey |
| **Marital status:** | Married |
| **Relation to Head of House:** | Head |
| **Home in 1940:** | Mount Holly, Burlington, New Jersey |
| **Map of Home in 1940:** | **Mount Holly, Burlington, New Jersey** |
| **Street:** | Pine Street |
| **House Number:** | 25 |
| **Farm:** | No |
| **Inferred Residence in 1935:** | Mount Holly, Burlington, New Jersey |
| **Residence in 1935:** | Same Place |
| **Resident on farm in 1935:** | No |
| **Sheet Number:** | 6B |
| **Number of Household in Order of Visitation:** | 144 |
| **Occupation:** | Proprietor |
| **Industry:** | Peat News W-k Gatherer |
| **House Owned or Rented:** | Rented |
| **Value of Home or Monthly Rental if Rented:** | 30 |
| **Attended School or College:** | No |
| **Highest Grade Completed:** | Elementary school, 7th grade |
| **Hours Worked Week Prior to Census:** | 53 |
| **Class of Worker:** | Working on own account |
| **Weeks Worked in 1939:** | 52 |
| **Income:** | No |
| **Income Other Sources:** | Yes |
| **Neighbors:** | View others on page |
| | **View others on page** |
| | **Name** **Age** |
| **Household Members:** | John Richardson 39 |
| | Helen Richardson 31 |

On the 1940 census, John Richardson listed his occupation as proprietor and industry as "Peat News W-k Gatherer." *Richardson family collection.*

as well as if not better than most of the Pineys, except for the old-timers, and he knew how to find the old-timers who lived in the remote areas of the Pines. Having that friendly air to him and knowing where to find many of the hermit-type Pineys deep in the pine hollows, he never had an issue gaining their trust and their business.

Ironically, Jack and his brothers would not call themselves Pineys, but Jack's children were proud to claim the title referencing their strong Piney heritage. On the 1940 census, John Richardson—located at 25 Pine Street, Mount Holly, New Jersey, at the age of thirty-nine—listed his job as "proprietor—peat gather," with the highest schooling completed being the seventh grade. Jack's knowledge of the various Pineycraft exceeded many a Piney because Jack had been in the business since the 1920s. He would routinely check Chatsworth bogs and other Piney hollows, knowing before many Pineys did when an item was ready for harvest. So one could say Jack was the ultimate Reluctant Piney.

A turning point in Jack's life was when he purchased the old Mount Holly Fairgrounds in 1945. The story goes that Jack was approached by two friends who were harness race drivers, and they asked, "John, do you want to go in on a three-way purchase of the property where the Mount Holly Fairgrounds is? It's up for sale." To their surprise, Jack replied, "Boys, I already purchased it for $10,000 in crisp $100 bills." The fairgrounds originally started out as an expansion of the Mount Holly Fair by the Burlington County Agricultural Society. In 1856, the society purchased "twenty-four acres on the Burlington Road at Woodpecker Lane, and constructed a half-mile race track, grandstand, and numerous exhibition buildings."

Up until 1926, the fairgrounds were a leading attraction for people across the region. The *Burlington County Times* reported, "For many years the Fair was the leading exhibition of its kind in the east and attracted thousands of visitors annually. Horseracing was a feature, the liberal purses attracting the owners of many of the fastest trotters and pacers. The governor of the state and many a prominent man were always present on 'Big Thursday.' US Vice President Sherman was once a guest and US President Woodrow Wilson attended several times." To illustrate how grand of an event the fair was to the state, the first passenger train ran from Camden to Mount Holly in October 1867 and carried passengers to the Mount Holly Fair, one of the "great fairs in New Jersey at the time."

Then for nearly twenty years, from 1926 to 1945, the fairgrounds were abandoned and the grandstands were torn down by local scavengers looking to either reuse the wood or create a souvenir representing a period of time

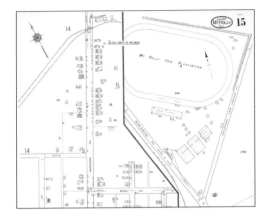

*Left*: Mount Holly, Burlington, New Jersey map by Sanborn Map Company, 1922. *Princeton University Online Library.*

*Below*: Mount Holly Fairgrounds, 1922. *Courtesy Mount Holly Historical Society.*

Grandstand - Mount Holly Fair 1922

that had great childhood memories for them. So when Jack took on the project of restoring it to its heyday, many thought it was quite an undertaking for an unproven young man. The grounds were in disrepair, and the horse racetrack had been used by the local high school football team for practices. A few years prior to Jack purchasing it, auto races were even held on the dirt track. And in 1944, there was a fire that destroyed the larger horse stalls just prior to Jack purchasing the property.

In quick fashion, Jack got the horse racetrack back in working order and moved his wholesale dried floral business to the fairgrounds. This is where

Mt. Holly Fair 1922

*Top*: Mount Holly Fairgrounds, 1922. *Courtesy Mount Holly Historical Society.*

*Bottom*: Mount Holly Fairgrounds in 1945, under ownership of John Richardson. *Richardson family collection.*

Jack developed a love for harness horse racing and, to a degree, gambling. After repairing the grounds and rebuilding the half-mile racetrack to racing conditions, naturally Jack brought back the weekly horse races on Sunday afternoons in Mount Holly. His son John Richardson still has a 1946 race certificate from the United States Trotter Association issued to Jack for the property listed as the Mount Holly Matinee Club. The timing was fortuitous, as New Jersey was once again falling in love with sport of horse racing.

THE UNITED STATES TROTTING ASSOCIATION

*This Certifies that* MT. HOLLY MATINEE CLUB,
IS A TRACK MEMBER IN GOOD STANDING OF THE UNITED STATES TROTTING
ASSOCIATION FOR THE YEAR AND AS SUCH MEMBER IS HEREBY SANCTIONED
TO CONDUCT A HARNESS RACE MEETING AT

1946

MT. HOLLY, NEW JERSEY

UNDER THE RULES AND REGULATIONS OF SAID UNITED STATES
TROTTING ASSOCIATION. THIS CERTIFICATE IS GRANTED AND ISSUED
PURSUANT TO THE CHARTER AND BY-LAWS OF THE
UNITED STATES TROTTING ASSOCIATION AND THE SEAL
OF THE ASSOCIATION IS HERETO AFFIXED BY ORDER
OF THE BOARD OF DIRECTORS.

Certificate sanctioning harness race meeting at Richardson-owned fairgrounds by the United States Trotting Association, 1946. *Richardson family collection.*

In 1945, the Thoroughbred Breeders' Association of New Jersey was established to "administer a New Jersey–bred incentive program for breeders, stallion owners and racehorse owners.…[It] hosts an annual awards banquet honoring Jersey-breds for outstanding performance, and publishes an annual magazine, *New Jersey Thoroughbred*." The *Mount Holly Herald* printed in an article about racehorses, "The revival of racing in New Jersey acted as a stimulant to the breeding industry and now Jersey provides a backlog of fine horses for each of the three licensed tracks within the state."

Anyone who did not know Jack could say it was a lucky chance, but others who knew Jack would say it was his business acumen that had him out front leading the resurgence of harness horse racing in New Jersey. Both Jack and his personal racehorse driver, Ed Kelly, became very prosperous, both owning racehorses and betting on the ones Jack owned over that ten-year period at the fairgrounds.

The transformation and reinvigoration of the fairgrounds was quite an accomplishment and required a lot of coordination and management on Jack's part. Remember, he was still dealing with Pineys from all across South Jersey bringing him loads of cattails on a daily basis. He would spread them out and place them on raised birch poles all around the entire racetrack to air dry before selling to the market. He had piles of birch poles, grapevine and other items staged on the grounds waiting to fulfill large orders. Once the order was completed, he had to load and deliver the Pineycraft items to end customers in places like Philadelphia and New York City. One building on the property at the fairgrounds was used to paint pinecones, birch whips

Mount Holly Race Track

*Above*: 1940s aerial photo of Mount Holly Fairgrounds. *Courtesy Mount Holly Historical Society.*

*Left*: John Richardson's horse Rufus pulling a sulky and driver Ed Kelly at the racetrack, August 1945. *Richardson family collection.*

and cattails in various holiday colors. Mostly this painting duty fell to his brother Lec Richardson.

In addition to his many business responsibilities, John was growing a family. Four years prior to purchasing the business from his mother in 1932, he had gotten married to eighteen-year-old waitress Helen Estelle (Myers) Richardson on September 15, 1928. Between 1928 and 1932, John was still figuring out what he wanted to be when he grew up. To support his

*Right*: John Richardson at Mount Holly Fairground stables. *Richardson family collection.*

*Below*: Birch poles, a Pineycraft item stored at the Mount Holly Fairgrounds. *Richardson family collection.*

new bride, he took a chauffeur job for a private family. That didn't last long before he and his wife decided to rent what at the time was called the Mount Holly Diner, located at the corner of Pine Street and Mill Street. Today, that building is gone and all that's left is a parking lot. John did the short order end, and Helen baked cakes and pies. They hired Penny Singleton to assist Helen in serving food to the customers. There was also a main chef and other waitresses on staff.

John had rented a home up until 1944 from a local farmer named Charley Fisher in Westampton, New Jersey. After buying the Mount Holly Fairgrounds, he moved the family—which included his new daughter, Pamela—to their new home. Jack was now roughly forty-four years old. He had his last child and only son, John M. Richardson, little Johnny, while he still owned the Mount Holly Fairgrounds. One day, sister Pam recalls, "I was at our neighbor's house at a birthday party for little Stanley Danser when Mom surprises me. She walks in with a bundled-up baby and said, 'It's your new little brother, Johnny.'" Johnny was born on August 7, 1950, Jack's forty-eighth birthday.

As a byproduct of the fairground races, local farmers and businesses benefited financially. The largest farm surrounding the fairgrounds was owned by the Danser family. Mrs. Danser (formerly Eleanor May Rhodier) had sold a piece of her property for $1,500 to a Mr. Fry, who wanted to stable his racehorses there prior to entering them in the Sunday races. Later, Mrs. Danser had another deed drawn up to sell another plot to Fry for the same

Out for a ride in Mount Holly. Seen here is John Richardson with his twin nephews, Dale and Gary, in the buggy behind horse Trigger in April 1945. *Richardson family collection.*

purpose. In an interview with ninety-four-year-old Mrs. Eleanor Danser, now Mrs. Rich, she recalls, "One Saturday on a lark I had given $6 to Bob to bet on a race for me, and the next day on my way to church he gave me $100. To my surprise, I won." Her husband at the time did not take kindly to gambling and wound up taking the winnings from Eleanor, and she never did get to spend any of it.

The Richardsons were welcomed to the neighborhood. Jack's children played with Mrs. Danser's children. She remembers having to hang wet towels in the front of the house to catch the dust particles that were kicked up by the horses on the neighboring track before they went into her home. And she thought it was funny that John Richardson was into selling weeds, too.

Alongside the horse-racing craze sweeping New Jersey, there was illegal gambling of all sorts. People took illegal bets for horse racing and playing the lottery in the form of slips in the Burlington County area. Mount Holly sits in the middle of Burlington County, and the area had a new prosecutor who was tough on illegal gambling. During his tenure, Harold T. Parker regularly made the headlines of the local *Mount Holly Herald* for his fight to clean up illegal mafia-related gambling, whether it be high-stakes poker—which moved from one location to another to avoid being detected, such as one of the small barns located at the Mount Holly Fairgrounds when Jack Richardson owned it—or a full-out illegal casino in neighboring Maple Shade. Likewise, Mount Holly had an illegal casino that was written about in Samuel Valenza Jr.'s book *The Secret Casino at Red Man's Hall*.

*Mount Holly Herald*, June 6, 1947: "Gamblers Jittery as Police Dragnet Closes; 10 Nabbed." *Microfiche, Burlington County Library System.*

Not everyone appreciated a good poker game, especially an illegal one. Jack's daughter Pam retells:

> *I was just a baby and we were living in a small house on the fairgrounds when one night there had been a poker game going in one of the small buildings on the property. There were people coming from New York and Pennsylvania, all bringing large sums of money. The standing house rule was all firearms were left at the table outside, just to keep everyone safe. Well, it seems that some of the nosey neighbors up on the mount saw the cars coming and going and people going into the darkened building, so they called the New Jersey State Police. When the raid happened, my dad, John Richardson, and Uncle Ernie went out a window and got away, but the rest of the men were busted. Mom said that Dad got into the house and told her to not turn on any lights to make it look like we were all sleeping.*

In another high-stakes poker game, there was an unsubstantiated rumor told by his brother Ernie that "Jack won the title to the Mount Holly Fairgrounds from the previous owner." His son, little Johnny, goes on to tell a story of his dad playing poker in his later years when he was seventy-five years old. Johnny retells, "Dad gives me a call late in the afternoon, saying he had a load of grapevine to go to Philly but he was running hot and asked me if I could run the load over without him."

It's safe to say that Jack's luck never left him in his lifetime. Always having luck on his side, as many a friend has said, gambling was an endeavor he dabbled in like many men and women of the era. He loved harness racing and high-stakes poker, and over the years, he won some and he lost some but always seemed to come out ahead.

In 1955, the United States stock market surpassed the 1929 pre-Depression high. A business developer approached Jack offering a large sum of money to purchase the fairground property. It's reported that Jack received between $100,000 and $150,000 in the real estate deal. Never a more dramatic landscape change has occurred than when they removed the Mount Holly Fairgrounds and nearby Mount Holly Airport, which both succumbed to the phrase "we paved paradise and put up a parking lot." Jack sold to developers who constructed the Fairgrounds Plaza Shopping Center, and the surrounding area became a housing development that replaced the airstrip and part of the fairgrounds. The photographs shown here illustrate the stages of development the fairgrounds property went through.

*This page*: Series of photos taken in 1955 of Mount Holly Fairgrounds right after it was sold to developers. *Courtesy Mount Holly Historical Society.*

Spring 1955

MT. HOLLY GARDEN STATE FAIR SEPT. 4 - 9

Spring 1955

Spring 1955

Notice the housing development had been constructed in this image, after which the shopping complex was built where the racetrack is shown here. *Courtesy Mount Holly Historical Society.*

Continuing his new love affair with harness racing, Jack eyed a 250-acre cow farm in the small town of Jobstown, Burlington County, with a price tag of $75,000. He moved in 1955, bringing his dried flower business and his family to the former Forrest P. Harker dairy farm on Jobstown-Jacksonville Road one mile west of Jobstown. Mrs. Durr, a woman from the neighboring farm across the street, described the Harker farm as "the most beautiful farm of its kind." It had a detached meadow off Route 537. A white picket fence surrounded the two-hundred-year-old brick farmhouse. Having no children to pass the farm on to, when Forrest Harker retired from farming he sold everything, including the farm equipment and land. Jack purchased the land and the buildings on it and converted the dairy farm to a horse farm. Seeing the need for a horse training track in the area, he installed a track and built a barn with one hundred stalls to board horses. However, he never raced horses here. That period of his life ended when he sold the Mount Holly Fairgrounds.

He continued working with local Pineys and running the dried floral business from the new farm in Jobstown from 1955 to 1957. Seen on page 82 is a picture of Jack on a riding lawn mower clearing an overgrown area for more staging ground for cut birch poles. You can't make it out in the picture, but he's probably chewing on a Phillie cigar. Never one to drink or smoke, he did love to chew on a Philadelphia Hand Made Phillie cigar. Later on, he'd wear a Phillies baseball cap during the day, and when he went out, he'd wear a different baseball cap that was more in the style of evening business casual. But he'd still be known to have a Phillie cigar in his mouth. In 2018, the last remnants of the farmhouse were knocked down, but you can still see the grading for the horse track Jack installed, and the property still has a lot of the Pineycraft items. Bittersweet is growing there where the birds helped disperse the seeds from bittersweet that Jack had collected and sold to the floral market in years past.

"Easy come, easy go," seemed to be a guiding principle of Jack during this period. He decided to sell the Harker farm and take the profit from the sale to build a stone ranch and horse stable on the detached meadow property along Monmouth Road. He moved the family to the smaller twenty-four-acre property in 1958 and stayed until 1960. The farm can still be seen in Burlington County today. The Once Upon a Time—John Richardson's 101 Items Wholesale Floral Supply came with him, but he lost his horse-training track.

In 1960, Jack had a rare lapse in luck when the Internal Revenue Service dealt him some misfortune in a questionable audit. Everything done in his day was done by cash. Pineys, especially in business deals, dealt in cash. Those living the Piney lifestyle, being reclusive and subsisting off the land, had very little reportable and taxable income. When he owned the fairgrounds, Jack's income tax filings were from the harness racing business only because there were no records of who brought in Pineycraft items or to whom the item of the day was sold.

Daughter Pam, who was in the kitchen at the time, describes the encounter:

> *There was an IRS agent named Pector, who was later proven to be corrupt. He sat in our kitchen and made up his own figures, saying that Jack and Helen owed the IRS over $12,000 in back taxes, but [he] was willing to take a payoff and forget everything if Jack would give him a certain amount of money. Dad didn't have that kind of money available, so the agent turned in his figures to the government. We were forced to sell their home, and that was the last time my parents ever owned a land deed.*

But Jack had a way about him to pick himself up when he hit a low. He never remained in a low place for very long. A neighboring farmer describes it as, "He had a habit. If he was down on his luck, he was always busy with his ambition and entrepreneurship and always had things to do to make

work. No matter what, you could always pull pinecones to make twenty-five dollars a day. No matter what, you could do something." And Jack did just that. He rented the old Armstrong farm from 1960 to 1965 in Jobstown that sat on the corner of Monmouth Road and Jacksonville Road.

On Monmouth Road, he rented for five years before moving again. At this property, he had a Piney family named Lewis build cedar boxes, and he

*This page and opposite*: Series of photos of Mount Holly Fairgrounds over the years: 1922, 1955, 1999 and 2019. *Courtesy Mount Holly Historical Society.*

built cedar boxes along with his kids and hauled them to the Philadelphia market by the truckload. He was always making cedar boxes, as he could always sell them.

People of his caliber were different, like the Robert H. Schuller quote: "Tough times don't last, tough people do." A story told by a Hornerstown, New Jersey resident reflects this attitude. "George Golff, just a little boy at

*Left, top*: John Richardson on a mower at the former Harker farm, July 1956. *Richardson family collection.*

*Middle and bottom:* Photos of the former Forrest P. Harker dairy farm on Jobstown-Jacksonville Road in 1957 (*left*) and 2019 (*below*). *Richardson family collection.*

*Left*: 2360 Monmouth Road, Springfield, New Jersey, where John Richardson built a stone rancher in 1958. *Author's collection.*

*Below*: Route 537 and Jobstown-Jacksonville Road in Jobstown, where John Richardson rented a small farm. *Author's collection.*

the age of twelve, remembers standing on his front porch in Hornerstown with his dad in 1936, and there coming down the main street was a brand-new 1936 Ford convertible with two coon dogs in the back, two beautiful women and a gentleman driving the car."

That gentleman was Jack Richardson. Even in the depths of the Depression, he still had what appeared to be a luxurious lifestyle. On any given day, he could be carrying a wad of $100 bills. Jack wasn't a philanthropic person, but his daughter said if a Piney family came in

A 1936 Ford convertible once owned by John Richardson. *Artwork provided by Hanna V. Lemke, also known as the artist milkdadd.*

and needed a small loan, he would help them out. He never cared a lot about money, but the things he cared for and worked with he liked to be of high quality.

Always use the best tool for the job, and Jack utilized the best tools in both his work life and personal life. His son recalls that his dad would purchase Austrian sickles and coated box nails by the fifty-pound box from Hobert's Browns Mills Supply. The sickles were used by hired hands—aka trusted Pineys—when they went to the pine creeks for cattails or to a field to harvest black bearded wheat. Some of the best craftsmanship in a steel cutting tool one could find at that price helped the pickers make quick work of a meadow full of cattails. The nails were used to assemble the cedar boxes that were used as planters.

One wouldn't offer up a coon dog as a tool, but if someone asked Jack what's the best tool for hunting raccoons, he'd say, "You gotta have a good coon dog from down south." Back in the late '70s and early '80s, raccoon hunting was akin to fox hunting on the level of grandeur. Sportsmen from all over came to the Pines to coon hunt. Fox hunting was prevalent in the Pines too, but that didn't appeal to Jack and his friends. You see, these fellas had interesting hobbies like playing poker and staying out late. Well, coon hunting is a night-owl hobby too, and Jack always spent a considerable amount of money on purchasing the best tool for the job. In the case of coon hunting, it was bluetick coonhound dogs.

*Top*: Brothers John and Ernest Richardson join others on Captain Dave Hart's boat the *Georgia Mann*. *Richardson family collection.*

*Middle*: John Richardson holding a coon dog on the far right of the image and August J. "Bob" Falkowski holding another coon dog on the far left in 1985. In the middle are two visiting coon hunters from Tennessee. *Richardson family collection.*

*Bottom*: Jack with a coon dog and raccoons on a Chevy half-ton '59 truck in Jobstown, New Jersey, 1961. *Richardson family collection.*

Even if he didn't have a lot of money at the time, he had to have the best dogs. Straight out of Virginia, these hunting dogs were known for their prowess in treeing a raccoon once they got the scent of one. Coon hunters hunt with coonhounds, and foxhunters hunt with foxhounds. Hunting for foxes and raccoons has all but become a thing of the past. Today, a neighbor would call the police if he saw men with flashlights traversing a field at 3:00 a.m.

One story many a friend of Jack Richardson heard over and over entailed an adventure with his competitor, his harness horse racing driver and his good friend Ed Kelly. The two men had made out late at night hunting raccoons in New Egypt, New Jersey, which had a lot of open space and farmland. There was an area at the edge of the southwest portion of the town off Brindletown Road that local hunters called Old Snag. Old Snag earned its name because of the twenty-foot wall of cat briers followed by a Pine Barrens swamp that was all but impossible to travel through on foot. John might have been fond of the area, as he was born not too far from there at Brindle Park near Brindle Lake. A hunting buddy and anonymous South Jersey farmer retells one of Jack's favorite hunting tales:

*There was a dog named Rock from Virginia who chased a coon right into Old Snag, and Jack and Ed lost the dog. Next thing you know, it's 3:00 a.m. and fog rolled in, and old Rock was still treeing a coon, but they couldn't get to the dog. Both guys get stuck in Old Snag and barely get out at 6:30 a.m. the next morning. So they left Jack's coat there for the coondog to come back.* [A good coon dog is trained to return to the scent of its owner when it gets separated.] *Jack and Ed come back the following day* [to Old Snag] *around 4:30 p.m., and sure enough they could still hear the coon dog treeing something. Several days after, on the fifth day, it was still treeing the raccoon, but they couldn't get to the dog. On the sixth day, there was silence—Jack had paid $3,100 for that dog, and they had lost him.*

*Now, like any good fishing tale, hunting tales have a small measure of an exaggeration, but here's how Jack told it. Some five years later, the same thing happens to them, they have a dog named Candy run across the same field into Old Snag. It seemed to be the same area, possibly the same tree. This time, the pair of hunters go in another way to find the dog Candy. They shine the flashlight up in the tree and shoot a coon that Candy had treed. Then they looked over to the tree next to it and see it had a skeleton of a dog with a collar at the base of the tree. They shined the light up to the top of the tree and seen a coon skeleton. Son of a gun if that wasn't ole Rock, who died treeing that raccoon who also succumbed to lack of water and starved in the tree, not being able to get away from the coonhound.*

Ocean County Natural Lands Trust signage along Long Swamp Road, New Egypt.
*Author's collection.*

A tragic ending that represents the value put on a good hunting dog.

In addition to Jack's unfortunate brush with the IRS, life was made tougher as the dried floral business began to wane from the competition with plastic flowers and fake plastic birch trees that had a longer shelf life than natural products. If a table bouquet of plastic flowers was set out at home and they looked a little dusty, they could be washed and rinsed, whereas a natural dried bouquet eventually left behind messy dried leaves on the table that needed to be cleaned up. Early on, the Richardsons were the only business in the market, but over the course of Jack's career, other copycat businesses popped up and fizzled out or struggled alongside him. The following story was known among the Pineys who went to Jack's regularly:

> *Jack and his driver* [were] *sitting at the counter at a local diner, the Garden State Diner in Wrightstown, New Jersey, and met a guy who was overly interested in what Jack did. Later, this guy—who was the Bond Bread delivery man—actually started a dried floral business of his own. It was rumored that this guy got into an accident and got a large settlement. It was cattail season, and Jack had a large order (100,000) to fill but had to wait for the cattails to dry out. Before they were ready, he gets a call that*

*the customer canceled the order. Had this order for cattails and didn't have a lot of competition, but the deal fell through, and they told him they were getting them from someone else. So who stole his order? Jack's discussing the mystery over with his brother, and someone tells them it was a guy by the name of Watts. Ernie yells out to Jack, "It's the damn bread guy from the diner." The Bond baker—the guy's name was Bud Watts. All that time, Jack was describing, in detail, his business to this guy who went on to copy his business.*

Other people in the business were old man Roman (aka Bucky Roman) in Whiting, New Jersey; Allyn Manufacturing Co. in Whiting; SBS Thayer Inc. from Quakertown, Pennsylvania; Bob Giordiano's Origin Marketing of Florence, New Jersey; Don "REDS" Cawley, inventor of wrapped grapevine wreaths, grapevine hearts and grapevine wall pocket wreaths; and two ladies, Lillian and Zee, from Browns Mills, New Jersey, who started a pinecone pricing war with Jack. These proprietors and a few other small-time buyers dealt in buying and selling of dried floral products. Some specialized in just a few Pineycraft items, whereas John Richardson had a larger array of goods. But even with stiff competition, Jack had the ability to see opportunities in his field where others didn't. He invented whole new markets for Pineycraft items that opened more opportunities for the Piney family to survive on.

From 1965 to 1994, the Richardson family traversed Monmouth Road and Sykesville Road, making a plus sign in Burlington County. Once they left Jobstown in 1965, they moved to 294 Sykesville Road (the creation of emergency 911 changed the original address from 58 Sykesville Road) in Chesterfield, which had a home, multiple horse barns and an old-fashioned milk house where the cedar box building part of the business was set up. Here Jack was renting from Bryce Thompson. The dried flower business started to improve. They started to sell more and more seasonal items like pepper grass and penny cress. Without realizing it, at the same time John McPhee published his book *The Pine Barrens* in 1967, which increased awareness of the fight to preserve the Pinelands. One can attribute the uptick in sales of natural dried floral decorations that the Richardsons were seeing to the popularity of this book, which detailed a few Piney families and the seasonal harvesting of items, such as pinecones, for the first time in print.

As luck would have it, Jack's son, after finishing his military service with the Air Force, moved to 396 Sykesville Road in Wrightstown in 1973–74. He talked his dad into moving north up the road from where he was to the larger farmhouse at 400 Sykesville Road a few years later, in 1979. This

John Richardson's residence at 58 Sykesville Road in Wrightstown, 2019. *Author's collection.*

was after Donald Emery, a previous tenant, vacated, leaving the house and fields empty. There was a lot of character and history in the main farmhouse, built in 1774, such as a coal-burning stove in the basement for heat. It was a perfect fit for Jack and the dried floral business. A businessman from Long Island named Fred Erb rented to the Richardsons before he died in a car accident and the farm was left to Bill Erb, who continued to rent to the family.

At this location, the business blossomed, and it was an all-time high in dried floral sales. Jack sold tractor trailers full of birch whips and hog brush. In the Northeast, from 1975 to 1990 there was a dried flower fad, and these were the golden years for Jack Richardson. You could sell almost any plant that could be properly dried and used in a floral arrangement. He had six hothouses full of cattails at a time. One of Jack's habits was to always have more cattails on hand than anyone else in the business. The Richardson Calendar worked like clockwork. This seasonal list of dried floral offerings gave consistent employment opportunities to Piney gatherers.

The cyclical downturn was ushered in by laws being passed by various governmental bodies and, thereafter, enforcement. In the late 1980s, the U.S. Department of Agriculture (USDA) sent agents out to the Richardson

*This page*: John Richardson's residence at 400 Sykesville Road in Wrightstown, 1992. *Richardson family collection.*

farm. Pam Richardson remembers, "One summer a federal agent from the USDA came to our farm to talk to my dad. He explained that if you gathered pitch pinecones off the Pine Barrens in South Jersey, the new trees would not grow. He tried to tell my dad that we would no longer be permitted to gather pinecones, and if we did and were caught, we would have to pay a fine. He then goes on to tell my dad how the seeds will not reproduce and the Pine Barrens will stop growing." Another part of the conversation might have been about shipping plant material from South Jersey when, in 1981, the height of the gypsy moth epidemic was hitting the Northeast. Pine and gray birch were a food source for gypsy moths, and Jack sent truckloads of birch whips around the country, which potentially could have spread the gypsy moth via cocoons or other stages of the moth.

*This page*: The booming farm at 400 Sykesville Road in Wrightstown, July 1981, showcasing piles of hog huck and birch whips. *Richardson family collection.*

Pam goes on, "My dad proceeded to tell him he didn't know where he had gotten his information, but he was way off base. The only way the seeds came out was through fire, which caused the cone to open. If no fire, then no seeds and no new trees would grow. The agent tried to argue with my dad but ended up being run off the property, [with my dad] telling him not to come back until he got smarter about how things are done around here."

This became the catalyst for local dried floral businesses similar to the Richardsons to import pinecones from China. The cones could be sourced more cheaply than paying the local Pineys to gather them and have them popped in a pinecone furnace. The Richardsons never imported pinecones; they always remained faithful to purchasing them from South Jersey Pineys.

*This page*: Winter of 1983 at the Richardson farm in Wrightstown showing a blanket of snow on piles of birch whips. *Richardson family collection.*

As the downward spiral continued into 1989–90, the increased international competition from imports and silk flowers had a devastating impact. Imported cattails from India and Chinese pinecones were hitting the market cheaper than they could be sourced from local New Jersey Pineys. Here we see the multinational enterprises in a world economy colliding with the Piney of South Jersey.

Characteristic of many young entrepreneurs who blazed trails in their specific industry, Jack's work ethic, trustworthiness and soft skills (or people skills) helped him to be profitable where others had failed. In his business dealings with Pineys, he never questioned their integrity, and they never mistrusted him. This enabled him to gain trust with this subpopulation of people who had a very high distrust for outsiders. An experience Jack had while coon hunting with some local Pineys reinforces the notion that his

*Top*: Winter of 1983 at the Richardson farm facing Sykesville Road with holiday cedar boxes stacked for sale. *Richardson family collection.*

*Middle*: Winter of 1983 at the Richardson farm. Young Jeff Richardson is in the foreground. *Richardson family collection.*

*Left*: Made-in-China products were fierce competitors to Pineycraft-made items, such as this grapevine wreath and birch bookends with fake red berries. *Author's collection.*

*Left*: John Richardson sitting in an old gray Ford work truck with daughter Pam in July 1992. *Richardson family collection.*

*Below*: Waning farm at 400 Sykesville Road in Wrightstown, fall of 1992, showing small piles of Atlantic cedar poles. *Richardson family collection.*

trust in Pineys was well placed. Gordy Lockwood recalls, "We were coon hunting with Jack one time, and he dropped his wallet in a ditch. I was behind him and found his wallet. I said, 'Jack, wait a minute, you dropped your wallet.' I gave Jack his wallet back, and Jack gave me a reward of $10, saying, 'I had $4,000 in that wallet. Thanks, Gordy.'" Everyone knew Jack carried around a lot of cash on any given day, yet no Piney ever tried to rob him. In later years, his daughter recalls that she noticed certain Pineys were less trustworthy than others and, over the years, seemed to get worse in their arithmetic. When a bunch of birch whips was supposed to be fifty, they would be passing off a bunch that contained forty-five. Jack would never question what the Pineys brought in.

In December 1994, John Richardson passed away. Much can be said about the man whose life's work meant so much to hundreds of Piney families, as well as the family he raised by pioneering a dried floral business that made wide trail blazes for other business-minded individuals to follow. Hopefully, his legacy was captured in these pages. A lot can be inferred by the inaction of the local government that did nothing to preserve the last place of residence of this American entrepreneur and leader in the dried floral industry and allowed his family's home to be destroyed. The 1700s farmstead was bulldozed in 2012. He may have moved to Sykesville Road, but his passion for horses that was cultivated in Mount Holly was always with him.

Friends and family still remember him and his brother Ernie for their unique sense of humor. The John Richardson Calendar of harvestable items from the Pines and surrounding farmland all but died with him. Even though we've attempted to document the 101 items of the Richardson dried floral business, no one is left who is dedicated to collecting and selling his robust catalogue of items. Some florists still to this day incorporate a Pineycraft item or two, mostly harvesting the items locally in New Jersey, but not to the degree the Richardson Calendar supplied.

At the farm, old friends John Richardson and Ed Kelley Jr. with John's grandson Jeff, circa 1980s. *Richardson family collection.*

If someone asked John what he sold, he had a song he would sing that listed

In Memory of
JOHN (Jack) RICHARDSON
Age 92 Years
Born
August 7, 1902
Died
December 18, 1994
Funeral Services
Thursday, December 22, 1994
at 11:00 A.M.
Tilghman Funeral Home
52 Main Street
New Egypt, N. J.
Clergy
Pastor Stephen Braddock
Interment
Jacobstown Baptist Cemetery

*Left*: John Richardson, a friend to many a Piney, passed away in Frankford Hospital in Philadelphia of kidney failure at age ninety-two. *Author's collection.*

*Below*: 400 Sykesville Road, where the early 1700s last residence of John Richardson was bulldozed. *Author's collection.*

everything he ever gathered and sold in alphabetical order. He's not here to sing that catchy song for us, and sadly, no one ever wrote it down. The Richardson Calendar business knowledge is all but lost to only a few remaining twenty-first-century Pineys. The people of New Jersey should be proud of the accomplishments of the Richardson family and the impact, along with local Pineys, they had on the nation's dried floral industry, which still today is reflected in the fresh-cut floral markets.

# Chapter 9

# *Are All Pineys the Same?*

Americans across the country regionally apply nicknames to certain segments of a local population. It's usually a geographical distinction that causes the populace to be isolated and therefore termed different. Sometimes, such terms are used in a derogative or ethnic way used to describe rural people. These labels are often adopted by the local people and brandished with a sense of pride that encapsulates their love of the culture, the time and the place they live. Arkansas has the Ozarks and the hill people; parts of Tennessee and West Virginia have hillbillies; the Blue Ridge Mountain range that passes through North Carolina and Virginia is known for the people of Appalachia, who are branded either as rednecks or hillbillies; and upstate New York has the Adirondack mountain people. New Jerseyans in South Jersey, particularly the Pine Barrens area, are labeled Pineys.

Those folks with the personal characteristics of what it is to be a Piney can claim the title too. It's like when you put on a cowboy hat and start to get a southern attitude. Well, the pine trees and the South Jersey wild areas are that metaphorical cowboy hat. Pineys are free-spirited, fiercely independent, outdoorsy, green pine–smelling fools. It is an easy leap to compare the American Indians' plight to the Pineys. In early America, the land defined the Indians; likewise, the million-plus acres of Pinelands define Pineys. For later generations of Pineys, like the rest of America, the car equaled independence. Ironically, it changed Pineys' lifestyle from less independent to more dependent on the outside world. That early pioneer spirit appeals to

A collage of Piney, hillbilly and redneck fan material. *Author's collection.*

people today, and in old Piney families, it still courses through their veins like the Batso or Wading River does the pines.

South Jerseyan Sarah Lewis, who lived from 1931 to 2017 and died at the ripe old age of eighty-five, went a step further and broke down the various types or groups of Pineys. She expressed her love and pride of the Pines in her "Piney Power" bumper sticker on her car. Not everyone shares her sentiment to encourage visitors or even to welcome outsiders to the Pines. It's the same personality type seen in past generations playing out the same old scene—an old-timer looking incredulously at a younger person when they're describing something that they know and love, as if to say, "you can't love that because we had it first and we loved it better then you could today." But even an outsider or a transplant to our area can look at this list and see for themselves where they fall. It doesn't take long for a person to become enamored with the Jersey Pines.

As Lewis is from a Piney clan that has deep roots in the sandy soil, who are we to disagree with her? Maybe one day someone will write a book on Granny Lewis's life. To say that she, with her fifth-grade education, had pearls of wisdom through her shared life experiences and stories is an understatement. And that those beneficial pearls should not be limited to a few family members is the main driver to pass on to you, the reader, in hopes that the illustrations (provided by Hannah V. Lemke, also known as the artist milkdadd) and descriptions included here enable you to see the Piney in yourself and that when someone asks, "Are you a Piney?" like Granny Lewis, you proudly can pronounce, "Why yes, I am!"

# The Company Piney

Vehicle driven: 1952 Chevy box truck with sides

Description: A leftover family in the Jersey Pines that worked for generations from one bust industry to another. Later, the local workforce was stabilized by farming. Both the owner of small and large farms and their loyal employees who worked the land are included here. Prime examples are the Ocean Spray folks who lived and died as company men. We're sure they did well for themselves and mean no negative connotations. Like the highly adaptive pine tree that makes up the Pine Barrens that suffers fire and is reborn and survives to regrow, the Company Piney has learned to do the same.

## The Conway Twitty Piney

Vehicle driven: 1973 Chevy Monte Carlo with windows tinted pink

Description: Conway Twitty was Granny's favorite guitar player. At Whitesbog Blueberry Festivals, she always liked the country and bluegrass bands, and as far as she was concerned, any person who could strum an instrument or carry a tune who lived in the Jersey Pines was a Twitty Piney.

## The Educated Piney

Vehicle driven: 1969 Cadillac DeVille convertible

Description: Those natives who were well off enough and had the smarts it took to go off to college. Sometimes they came back and stayed in the Jersey Pines, and lots of times they just visited.

## The Firefighter Piney

Vehicle driven: 1970 Dodge New Jersey Forest Service truck

Description: Fire and the Pines go together like peanut butter and jelly, and the same could be said about the South Jersey firefighter. Whether fighting wildfires year-round protecting their neighbors or fighting fire in their own backyards, their sense of service to the region is admirable. This was not always a full-time paying job, but it is full-time work when a fire catches. The volunteer firemen and the fire stations supporting them become twenty-four-hour fixtures of the Piney landscape.

## The Hunter Piney

Vehicle driven: 1959 F1000 Chevy half-ton truck with dual headlights
Description: Many a shotgun-toting young man came to the Jersey Pines to hunt game animals like ducks, deer, foxes and bobwhite quails. They established hunting clubs and had hunting cabins in their territories and came down and stayed during the hunting season. The love of the land eventually gets a strong hold on many of these outsiders and turns them into insiders and year-round residents. Not to be confused with the Woods Piney, this is more of an adjective to describe the Piney who is attuned to the seasonal rhythms of the Pines. Many of those hunters adopted other work to support their love of hunting, with some even becoming pinecone pickers. Note author John Stinton in the book *Pinelands Folklife* first described in general terms someone who decided to stay in the Pines: "those who could live within the seasonal rhythms of the place."

# THE OUT-OF-TOWN PINEY WITH BOAT SLIP

VEHICLE DRIVEN: 1970s Mercedes Benz G-Class SUV with trailing boat
DESCRIPTION: Lots of folks who are rich enough to have a second home located in the Jersey Pines tend to have money for a boat as well. Whether you like it or not, we all came to the area at one time or another. The closeness to Philly and New York has had a major influence in shaping the area. A few of those are proud to wear the title of Piney just like the rest of us, and the rest of us welcome them to it.

# THE PATRIOTIC PINEY

VEHICLE DRIVEN: 1940s USMC with machine gun
DESCRIPTION: The Jersey Pines has a large chunk of it contained behind big government fences where thousands of men and women are trained to be in the armed forces. A lot of those folks who came to the area from around the United States retired in New Jersey, happy and content to live in their adopted state, finding solace in the open space and the many opportunities to fish, trap and hunt in the Pines.

# THE RELUCTANT PINEY OR WOODS PINEY

VEHICLE DRIVEN: 1972 Ford F100 truck

DESCRIPTION: This type was never really described by Granny Lewis, so the author here is injecting his interpretation to describe Granny herself. Poor enough to afford a tub of lard and a loaf of white bread, this Piney would make lard sandwiches for lunch. The Woods Piney depended on the woods to provide the family with a wage to live by. Whether the men ran beat-up pickups through the woods looking for scrap junk cars or were hauling a load of pinecones from the plains, you betcha they didn't care what you called them. With fried snapper meat from snapping turtles caught fresh out of the flowing creeks or deer shot year-round to keep the fridge full, this Piney did what he could to get by. Certain times of the year—especially winter, when the grasses that fetched twenty-five cents a pound in the summer were out of season—were toughest on those who depended on a cyclical land harvest. These Woods Pineys survived on their knowledge of the land. And when they went to work, no matter where they were heading to or what they were doing, whether it was trapping, junking or cutting a Pineycraft item, it was always "heading out to the woods" or "tomorrow we're going to the woods." There are many reasons for the word "Reluctant" to be used to describe these Pineys. As the times were changing and full-time employment took them out of the woods, they were reluctant to go, but progress caught up to them. They were reluctant to leave the generational life of woods work but knew they had to adapt or become extinct. Note some would say there are many other reasons for this type of Piney to be reluctant, but we will let you find all of them out on your own.

# THE SAMMY DA CLAMMY PINEY

VEHICLE DRIVEN: 1964 panel truck

DESCRIPTION: These are the Pineys who came from the ocean towns and sold great seafood, especially oysters and clams. Their living wages were earned with the help of the bay, so they were officially recognized as Baymen. Some even say if you live near Route 9 and east you're not a Piney but a Bayman. When they weren't living off seafood, they farmed the bay meadows for salt hay and eel grass and built one-of-a-kind boats, making them highly sought after boat builders. Many of the Baymen were expert duck decoy carvers and served as guides for sportsmen seeking respite from city life and adventure hunting waterfowl and shorebirds like the rail along the Jersey Shore and particularly Barnegat Bay in sneakbox-type boats.

# THE TREEHUGGER PINEY

VEHICLE DRIVEN: 2000 Prius

DESCRIPTION: Someone who takes a photo of Lake Absegami and captures the pristine landscape and never wants to see it altered, just like a snapshot in time. Today, we call them environmentalists and conservationists. Many flocked to the area and continue to do so seeking glimpses of the unique flora and fauna. Possibly without their help, we wouldn't have the Pines we have today.

# *Pineys' Dirty Little Secret Explained*

With every fairy tale that starts with "once upon a time," like John Richardson's business Once Upon a Time—101 Items, there are some half-truths mixed in with facts to make the legend that much more memorable. Did you catch a few unknown truths about the Piney life as you were reading this book? What was the one huge revelation that would make it impossible to live that lifestyle today? Some Pineys might say "don't give it away," like the locals who don't want more people knowing how beautiful it is in the Pines. If you tell everyone how peaceful and wonderful it is to live down here, everyone who hears you will come down, and the darn tourists will overcrowd us. And that'll drive the price of everything up, including our houses, and we'll be forced to move away. People have a tendency to know when they have a good thing going and shush everyone else who wants to bring awareness to it.

But that's not the main dirty little secret. You might have picked up on it in chapter 9, where the life history of John Richardson was laid out. If you remember, the law caught up to Jack in 1960. Still haven't figured it out yet? Remember, Jack carried around cash in the amount of $4,000 in his wallet, sometimes even more. And all the other dried floral buyers of the day did the same. Pineys told us that the Quakertown, Pennsylvania buyer Robert Thayer had $15,000 in cash on him at all times, similar to Jack. The reason behind this was that they bought and paid for Piney goods in cash. It was mostly an underground economy in a black market, really a green/brown market that moved these products from the Pines to city windowscapes.

Therein lies the conundrum. What enabled the Woods Pineys to continue living off the land and support their families was a constant cash flow from a landscape full of products. This particular lifestyle that the Reluctant Piney lived was balanced by a strict shoestring budget. Today, to live their lifestyle of hunting and fishing part of the year and picking pinecones and cutting sweethuck the rest of the year would be near impossible unless you had another form of income like a large nest egg in the bank, as the dried floral industry literally dried up in the early 1990s. (Interesting note: as this was being written in 2019–20, there was a resurgence in the interest of dried flowers for home design. Maybe it's coming back into fashion.)

You learned about the Pineys' reclusiveness in chapter 1. That reclusiveness not only stemmed from being afraid of the aftermath of the Goddard report and subsequently being labeled inbred morons but also of other public authorities. The persona of Tony from *The Sopranos* might be a good comparison here where a family man turns to crime to support the family. Pineys continued to cut birch at places like Weymouth and Wharton State Forest because for generations they had been taught by family to go to those sites.

In addition to watching for a ranger or a game warden, they were either unaware of the fact that selling their Piney goods to a middleman was frowned upon or they were willfully ignorant of the non-cutting laws on public lands. That mere fifty dollars for a ten-hour day spent on the plains of Warren Grove picking pinecones in the snow was a straight hard-earned fifty-dollar bill in your pocket that helped put food on the table.

The other attractive part to working the cycle of the Richardson Calendar was that many Pineys were already getting some sort of government aid. People kept to themselves, but the Pineys knew who was getting government aid and who continued to work under the table making a living wage from the woods. These were veterans, people with disabilities, temporarily unemployed workers, retirees and welfare recipients who worked the Richardson Calendar too. Can we blame them?

If we look at their actions with our twenty-first-century lens, maybe we would and maybe we wouldn't condemn their behavior. To be fair, only a few secondhand stories were told during the information-gathering part of this book project about a family that was double dipping. And just as many stories were told of some Piney who already had a normal forty-hours-a-week job who moonlighted working nights and weekends collecting pinecones in the dead of winter to put food on the table. Today, some would call it working a side hustle. But no doubt it was definitely better than the outsiders who went into the Pines to exploit the remoteness by capturing highly sought after and rare species of snakes and reptiles and selling them illegally to the highest bidders. And other outsiders conducted the same illegal activity by digging up pitcher plants and sundews that have a high resale value to collectors, sometimes ending up at area flea markets like South Jersey's largest outdoor flea market, the Columbus Farmers Market.

Certainly, this revelation should tarnish some of the romanticism of the Piney subsistence lifestyle. Granny Lewis (Sarah Lewis), who we talked about in chapter 8, was a prime example. She was a Piney and was married to a Piney. She never had full-time employment, but boy could she pick blueberries; there was never a faster picker in the patch. She never paid into Social Security her entire adult life until her husband passed, and the government made her work a number of years after the legal age to retire before being able to collect Social Security.

We've come full circle with the term Piney. Hopefully, someone will update the Wikipedia citation for the word "Piney (Piney Pine Barrens resident)," where it's still described as a derogatory term. Today, if you travel down one of the many paved roads that lead into the Jersey Pines, watch for plainclothes Pineys at places like Hot Diggidy Dog in Chatsworth or the Lower Bank Tavern. It will be hard to spot them unless they have a bumper sticker on their pickup trucks. But if you're at Sweetwater Bar & Grill and find yourself enjoying a beer or two, you just might be a Piney and you don't know it! Just like the paint cracking and fading away on the sides of the Hedger House, those Reluctant Pineys are beginning to leave our collective memories, so please pour an extra round at the local bars in their honor, and those establishment walls will record your adventures like the Hedger House's walls did before.

This is just one telling of several unknown life histories woven together into one story, representing one type of Piney, that Reluctant or Woods Piney. After digesting what you read, can you not walk away with a newfound respect for those country bumpkins? I invite you to ask yourself, "How come there is no Piney museum preserving the culture the Pineys built around harvesting dried floral arrangements?" South Jersey Pineys deserve to be treated better in our history. Or better yet, admit to yourself that there is a type of Piney that you yourself identify with. At a minimum, I hope these pages and these pictures immortalize the culture of the Reluctant Piney. My last parting words are from Granny Lewis. Remember to say it with pride and say it loud: "I'm proud to be a Piney from my nose down to my hiney!"

# Typical Piney Family, Example 1

## THE LEWISES

The Lewis family owned forty acres of farmland on Pemberton Road in Pemberton, New Jersey. Samuel NMN Lewis (August 1, 1896–January 1954) and wife Cora Maxwell Lewis (June 1896–February 1960) had four children together, oldest to youngest in order: Dorothy, Samuel, Joseph and Elsie. All of them had children, and the Lewis family tree has blossomed in South Jersey since the nineteenth century through to today in the twenty-first century.

From humble beginnings, the two sons, Samuel Lott and Joseph Roy, who were known mostly by their middle names, never got around to adapting to societal standards of the twentieth century where the man married and was supposed to get a steady forty-hour-week job. Maybe it was due to the lack of education—neither could read or write—or maybe it was from being raised during the Great Depression. Their folks, Samuel and Cora, never lost any money in the New York Stock Exchange, as their only possessions were farm equipment and four farmhands in the form of children. Being a farmer teaches a person to be resourceful, as you never have enough money to go out and buy the best tool for the job, nor do you have the extra money to hire outside help. What the family did have was food on the table, from canning vegetables to baking bread from scratch. One thing the Great Depression taught families was to be independent, as resources were slim for everyone, not just the dirt farmers.

Both Lott and Roy (again, they used their middle names versus given names) left the farm first, while their sisters Dorothy and Elsie stayed with

*Left*: Samuel NMN Lewis with a horse used to plow the farm fields. *Author's collection.*

*Above*: Joseph Lewis. *Author's collection.*

their mother, Cora, until her death in the early 1960s. After the farm was sold and their parents died, the siblings kept close to one another. Usually, when one moved to a town the other siblings would move to the same town or a neighboring town. They preferred seclusion from outsiders. Lott at one time lived at the edge of an old bog off Route 70 in Pemberton Township, and Roy today would be what Myers Briggs calls an extreme introvert. He liked lots of space away from neighbors, and his last residence in Browns Mills provided remoteness, as it was situated along the old Pennsylvania Railroad Kinkora Branch tracks on Junction Road.

Lott and Roy started picking pinecones and the like after they left the farm. They brought along their children and showed them the ropes. Lott loved to pick pinecones or cut sweethuck, whereas his little brother Roy would rather go junking for cash in the pines and haul scrap metal to one of the local junkyards at the time. There was an endless supply of stolen and or abandoned vehicles that were dumped in the pines, and sometimes they had been set on fire. Scrapping, like cutting firewood in the winter months, was a fill-in job for part of the year for both of them when they weren't picking Pineycraft items.

Heck, Roy and his brother-in-law Walter once had an odd job on Fort Dix, from which they were promptly fired for picking up used brass shells in bags. At the time, the military would leave mounds of bullets, some

| LEWIS | Joseph "Roy" Lewis- *Husband* 1928- 1987 | Sarah Marie (Britton)Lewis- *Wife* 1931- 2017 |
|---|---|---|
| | Sarah L. Britton- Daughter 1953- 1973 | |
| | Wayne "Butchy" Britton- Son 1954- 1975 | |
| | Joseph Edward Lewis- *Son* 1956- present | Charlotte (Emery)Lewis- *Wife* 1956- present |
| | Linda "Doll" Lewis- Daughter 1963- present | |
| | Patrick Lewis- *Son* 1967- 2017 | Cathy Egenlauf -*longtime partner* 1952- present |
| | Robert Lewis- *Son* 1970- 2012 | April Jean Stevenson- *longtime partner* 1965- 2004 |

*Left*: Cora Maxwell Lewis standing in the doorway of the Pemberton farmhouse. *Author's collection.*

*Above*: Joseph Lewis family tree. *Author's collection.*

in clips of six, out in the pinewoods training areas, and the two of them decided to collect some and sell them for scrap. That's probably where Roy first started his love of scrapping. Scrapping part time complemented the Richardson Calendar of 101 dried floral items because when you were out in a sandpit looking for a place to cut sweethuck, you'd come across an abandoned car or two. Usually, someone who stole a car would torch it and leave it out in the pines. Well, Roy always had a pickup truck, and on the back of that pickup truck was a set of torches with an acetylene tank and oxygen tank that he kept filled with weekly runs to a guy in Lakewood, New Jersey. He used the torch to cut a vehicle up into smaller pieces and used his 1950s flatbed truck's lift gate to push the old scrap vehicle onto the truck by backing into a tree or manually hoisting the scrap car frame up onto the truck bed using a Come-Along ratchet. Roy struggled all his life with asthma. He was known to use an old Piney home remedy: a pillowcase stuffed with old field balsam/blossom or sweet everlasting, as it was supposed to help with breathing issues like nasal congestion and asthma to enable a person to sleep. But with no fanfare, every day he'd still put in twelve hours in the plains pulling pinecones if he had to.

The Lewis brothers used the Richardson Calendar to collect items throughout the year and sell to the dried floral markets, all the while supporting both their families. Sister Elsie's husband, Walt Hertell, on

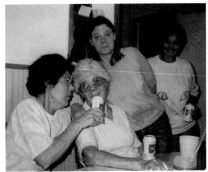

*Left*: Samuel Lewis. *Author's collection.*

*Right*: Lewis brothers' sisters. *Author's collection.*

| LEWIS' continued | Samuel Lewis- *Husband* 1925- 1992 | Samuel Lott Lewis- Husband 1925-1992 | Lenore Ann (Mize) Lewis- Wife 1927-1989 |
|---|---|---|---|
| | | Fredrick Grant Mize- Son 1944-2007 | |
| | | Brenda (Lewis) Raines- Daughter 1959- present | |
| | | Samuel J. Lewis II- Son 1957- present | |
| | | Sandra Kay (Lewis) Kloos - Daughter 1955- 2014 | |
| | Elsie Lewis- *Sister* 1933- 2019 | Elsie (Lewis) Hertell- Sister abt 1933- 2019 | |
| | | Rachel Hertell Hopper- Daughter 1957-2019 | |
| | | Ronnie Hertell- Son 1963- present | |
| | | Walter "Bug" Hertell- Son 1959- present | |
| | Dorothy Lewis- *Sister* 1923- 2004 | Dorothy Lewis 1923- 2004 | |
| | | Annie Lewis- Daughter 1959- present | |
| | | Johnny Chambers- Son 1948- present | |

Samuel Lewis family tree. *Author's collection.*

occasion helped out in the woods when he was out of work too. But the Lewis brothers never aspired to full-time professions other than woodsmen. Lewises had worked for John Richardson in various capacities since about the 1940s. When John got an order for a specific item, he would let the Lewises know what he needed, and they would get it. And if he needed a few Pineys to go cut a farm crop like bearded wheat or yellow yarrow, he'd hire one or two of the Lewis sons. All of them at one time or another worked for John cutting a specific plant or working on the farm. There was little Sammy, son of big Sam, and of Joe's children, the boys who worked for Richardson

All hands on deck to clean birch whips at Junction Road in Browns Mills. *Author's collection.*

were: little Joe aka Punk, Pat and Bobby. The following Lewis generation of great-grandkids worked the woods to varying degrees until the dried floral business and the old-timers who ran the industry passed away.

It wasn't just the men who worked in the Pines. The Lewis women worked the Pineycrafts as well. Big Sam and his wife, Lenora, worked for twelve hours a day building cedar flower planters when they were young. They built cedar boxes from Atlantic white cedar year-round at their private residences and at the Richardson residence. The last place they built boxes together was in the repurposed old Richardson chicken coop that was turned into a small factory of cedar planters at 400 Sykesville Road in Wrightstown in the 1980s.

Roy's wife, Sarah, never hesitated in following her husband into the woods, being from Piney stock herself. Sarah, who also went by her middle name of Marie, was apt to make old-fashioned sun tea the night before they went out picking for the day so that they had iced tea when they got home. But both Roy and Marie worked the woods together. Pulling a truckload of pinecones or filling an order for one hundred bales of grapevine, they did it as a team. They'd haul the children with them. The only time Marie didn't go was when there wasn't room in the truck. Now the kids could still go even if there wasn't room in the cab of the truck, as they could ride on the back. Roy applied the earlier lesson learned from his farmer parents that many hands make the load lighter and everyone needs to earn their keep. Even at a very young age, the children were out there, as there was no paying a babysitter. Little Joe Lewis got lost in the woods when they were cutting sweethuck one time, so after that, Marie had a rope tied to him

Brothers Pat and Bobby Lewis shown here cleaning cattails at Junction Road in Browns Mills. *Author's collection.*

until he was old enough to stick to her and not wander off exploring. Little Joe remembers another time when his mom and dad got in an argument because she took longer than usual at Allyn's Manufacturing in Whiting to get the check for the pinecones. See, they had made a mistake in the office and paid her for ten bags of pinecones when they only brought in eight. She got razzed for that for months after. Honest as the day's tea was sweet.

The head cook was Marie. A funny story retold by her eldest son, Joseph Lewis, tells of how much in charge she was of the household. Joseph says:

> *One time when I was young, I remember my dad and his brother-in-law Walt going fishing for bluefish. They got lucky and had a good catch. Feeling good about themselves, they stopped at a liquor store and got beer on the way home and forgot about putting the fish on ice. Well they came home and walked into the house with the fish and beer. And promptly Mom tossed them out of the house and threw the beer and spoiled fish out the door to boot. She wasn't an excitable woman, but that got a rise out of her that day and a scolding for the two men. Boy, she was mad, but usually she was the one that kept the peace. Piney stock of Marie came from the Britton side. Her mom and dad lived in various shacks without electric or any modern conveniences at places like Success Lake in Colliers Mills, Jackson. One time her dad, Joseph Britton, had a job watching over cranberry bogs in New Egypt, which claimed to be the first place to make and can cranberry sauce.*

Roy died in 1987, and Sarah Marie would outlive him by thirty years, passing in 2017 but never remarrying. She always carried a keychain with his name on it.

# Typical Piney Family, Example 2

## THE CAWLEYS

The Cawley family shared many of the same traits of other Piney families like the Lewises in Appendix A. The patriarch of the family was Donald, nicknamed Reds Cawley. His Piney résumé of living in the woods for sixty years started when he was just a kid and friends with John Richardson, who went on to be a big-time seller of Piney products to the Philadelphia and New York markets. Reds was born in Jobstown, New Jersey, but throughout his life, he, along with his wife, whom he met and fell in love with as a teenager in 1961, and their subsequent family, lived in various places in Chatsworth and Burlington City, New Jersey. They were always in or nearby the Pines.

He cut cattails in the dirt, pulled pinecones, cut wild grasses like pepper grass, cut laurel and gathered many other items that others consider to possess the quintessential Pineyness. He partnered with a few guys from Allyn's Manufacturing in Whiting, New Jersey, in the early 1980s and formed the dried floral business Origin Marketing. Prior to that, he and his wife, Alice, and two sons worked the seasonal Richardson Calendar of items and sold to Richardson and other buyers in the area.

Typical of most married Pineys, both the man and woman worked in the woods. Just like the Lewis brothers' wives, Alice was always by her husband's side picking and did her fair share of picking in the woods on her own when the children were in school. Alice tells a story of having a run-in with a dirt bike rider along the railroad tracks in Burlington who almost ran her over as she was out by herself cutting brown burr. Unlike elkshorn or buttons that

Reds Cawley at a hunting cabin in September 1972 with son Judd Cawley and pelts. *Cawley family collection.*

Reds Cawley at a hunting cabin in September 1972 with his hunting dog. *Cawley family collection.*

| CAWLEYS | Donald 'Reds' Cawley- *Husband* 3/23/1939- 7/30/2013 | Alice Horton Cawley- *Wife* 2/16/1944- present |
|---|---|---|
| | Judd W. Cawley- *Son* 9/13/1968- present | Cheyenne D. Cawley- *Judd's daughter* 11/09/1991- present |
| | Jake W. Cawley- *Son* 6/21/1976- present | |

Reds Cawley family tree. *Author's collection.*

grow on rattlesnake ground, brown burr grows on sandy, firm soil, so she felt more comfortable and less fearful of running into a snake. When their two boys, Judd and Jake, were in school and Reds was out working in the woods, she would stay close to home and work a few hours in between her responsibility to the kids. Alice could have their 1970s green Ford station wagon filled with brown burr and still pick up the boys after school.

Pineys were resourceful, and some had that entrepreneurial spirit to forge out on their own. Reds was also a well-known South Jersey trapper. In 1978, the *Burlington County Times* wrote a piece on him titled "The Trapper's Art Is an Ageless Tradition." He not only trapped furs but also coon hunted and was an avid deer hunter and fisherman. He passed this tradition on to his sons, who passed it on to their children. Between Reds and his son Judd—who goes by several nicknames, including Outlaw and Indian and has a tattoo that says "Piney Power" with the Jersey Devil on his back—there is over one hundred years of trapping experience. Similar to the Lewises' junking or scrapping, the Cawleys' trapping served as another source of income when they weren't working the Pineycrafts. Also, both scrapping and trapping could be done year-round in addition to picking seasonal items.

In the downtime, like many other Piney families, music was used to lift the spirit from days and nights toiling in the woods—sometimes twelve hours straight pulling pinecones, from sunup to sundown. Reds was self-taught and played the guitar. Like many a Piney, he loved country western music. They say that when he sang he sounded just like Waylon Jennings, who was his favorite country western singer. He even bought a white left-handed Gibson guitar to play—that's how much he liked Waylon. He'd sing one of his favorite Waylon songs, "Don't You Think This Outlaw Bit's Done Got Out of Hand." Maybe Reds associated with the outlaw and fighter

A truck loaded with Pineycrafts from 1972 Reds Cawley's and friend Roger's families. *Cawley family collection.*

persona of Jennings. When he was younger in the 1950s, Reds was a little like what Waylon sang about being "rough and rowdy" and would never shy away from a fight. This would lead him to eventually get to know the legendary Rubin "Hurricane" Carter, who asked him to spar in Trenton. Probably one of the reasons for Carter to pick a streetfighter like Reds was that he was also a lefty or southpaw. Some of you might know Rubin Carter today by the popular Bob Dylan song "Hurricane," which was released in 1975 and eventually contributed to Carter being released from jail in 1985. Reds and his friends usually played in a friend's basement or someone's den. Just the way they liked it—belting out country tunes in a smoke-filled room surrounded by hunting and woods friends.

*Left*: Judd Cawley's Piney Power and Jersey Devil tattoos, inked when he was eighteen. *Author's collection.*

*Below*: Reds Cawley, a noted left-handed musician who was self-taught, seen here playing guitar at his friend Jim's hunting cabin. *Cawley family collection.*

Legends all must come to an end in order for their life stories to become legends. It's interesting to note that Reds was first introduced to the Pine Barrens book that was said to have saved the area in the early 2000s. Reds was a ferocious reader all his life, atypical of most Pineys, even though he only finished the eighth grade. In his seventies, his wife, Alice, bought John McPhee's book *The Pine Barrens* at Buzby's General Store in Chatsworth. Reds read about twenty pages of the book and tossed it in the waste can. When asked by his son why he did that, he said, "I don't think any of that is authentic. I'd rather read a comic book!" And just so you know, Reds never read comic books.

# Richardson Calendar

The Richardson Calendar was named after John Richardson, who pioneered and dominated the Pineycraft market after purchasing the family business from his mother in 1932 and successfully running it for a span of sixty-two years. The intimate knowledge of many of the Pineycraft items contained in the Richardson Calendar has been in the American lexicon since precolonial days, consisting of over one hundred items that grew wild in the Pine Barrens area.

### Schedule of Harvest Season
#### YEAR-ROUND*
Sassafras poles, birch whips and poles, super birch, cedar poles, laurel, sphagnum moss, pinecones, grapevine, Atlantic white cedar tree-boxes, sweethuck, hoghuck, catbrier
*many of these items can be done year-round, but it was always easier after the leaves fell off to gather them; for instance, sweethuck and birch whips both needed leaves removed

#### SPRING MONTHS OF MARCH, APRIL AND MAY
Shepherd's purse, penny crest, mustard grass, wisteria vines, fluffy grass, dock, Sphagnum moss (as early as February/March but year-round too)
Cultivated items: N/A

John Richardson, July 1992, 400 Sykesville Road farm. *Richardson family collection.*

SUMMER MONTHS OF JUNE, JULY AND AUGUST

Week of Memorial Day Cattailing occurred (June 21–26), pepper grass (June 21), foxtails, cats paws (July–August), sea statice (July–September), bayberry (July–September), coffee grass (August–September), plumes (August–September), elkshorn, buttons, orange bud, tansy (common yarrow), Queen Anne's lace, fingerweed, miniature wild oats, types of goldenrod, ironweed, Joe pye, milkweed, mullein, mustard grass, bloodroot, rose spirea, snake weed, thistles, pinecone on a stick, pearly everlasting*
*Pearly everlasting is a wild Pennsylvania/Maine-grown item used in floral bouquets
Cultivated items: yellow yarrow (June–July), bearded wheat, baby's breath, German statice, English statice, cockscomb, timothy, orchard grass (grows wild as well), dried nigella flower (August–September), caspia, straw flower, globe thistle, larkspur, sweet Annie*
*Sweet Annie is cultivated but also cut wild in Pennsylvania

FALL MONTHS OF SEPTEMBER, OCTOBER AND NOVEMBER

Sea statice (July–September), plumes (August–September), bayberry (July–September), coffee grass (August–September), fern center (October), brown burr (October), turkeybeard (October), bell grass, old field balsam/blossom

(September–October), snake grass, sweet gum twigs, sweet gum balls, bog rush, heather, red cedar with berries, horsemint, Indian grass, acorns-on-a-stick, pampas grass, bananacones, strogus cones, candy pods, elephant grass, winterberry, witch hazel, bittersweet, rice crispies
Cultivated items: Eucalyptus, purple salvia

### Winter months of December, January and February
Sphagnum moss (as early as February–March but year-round), holly swags, mistletoe, crow's foot, standing pine, bird's nest, bear brush
Cultivated items: N/A

# Example Stories Contained in Forthcoming Book

## The Richardsons' Piney Calendar: A Field Guide to the Flora of the Pines

Many stories of those interviewed who guardedly provided anecdotal Piney "picking" experiences from the twentieth century are retold here for the first time in print. The following pages are a sampling of real-life personal stories from the Reluctant Pineys who traveled on the same dirt road right back to Jack Richardson and the little farmstead located at 400 Sykesville Road in Wrightstown, New Jersey. A full-length field guide titled *The Richardsons' Piney Calendar: A Field Guide to the Flora of the Pines* is in the works.

Not all of these items are found in the Pine Barrens, and not all of these items are unique to New Jersey. Some are found deep in the heart of the Pines only and go by many names. In the field guide book, I will provide the common names for each item, the name the Pineys used or names that Jack Richardson made up and the scientific Latin names. For example, an item that grows deep in the Pine Barrens is known by Pineys as elkshorn and its common name is gold crest, but the true scientific name is *Lophiola aurea*.

As a disclaimer, I want everyone reading this book to know the New Jersey statutes when referencing collection of plant material. I do not encourage illegal activity in any form on public or private land. This field guide was not written with the intention to promote harvesting of plants for personal use or resale. The use of said guide is to enrich the user's experience when encountering a Pineycraft item in the wild.

# GRAPEVINE: BALES, TREES AND WREATHS

### TOOLS OF THE TRADE

For grapevine wreaths, the picker used a pair of sharp craftsman clippers to cut the vine at ground level and then would have to pull straight down from the tree to pull the vine out of the upper tree limbs. The larger and older the vine, the harder it was to pull out of the tree without bringing tree limb fragments with it. Young grapevine was easier to roll into a wreath in the spring and summer, when it still had to have the leaves removed by picking them clean by hand. Different buyers wanted the bales differently. One buyer bought only wrapped grapevine wreaths, whereas others bought wreaths that were tied up with farm baling twine (four pieces applied at 12, 3, 6 and 9 on a clock). Also, large consolidated bales were sold that were nothing more than a bundle of grapevine, whereas a wreath had a set amount of grapevine in it to make up the perfect door decoration. Grapevine trees could also be made and sold using an upside-down tomato cage.

### PERSONAL ACCOUNT

Henry Stubbs, an African American gentleman from Camden who was a bricklayer, pulled bales of grapevine instead of wrapped wreaths. He did this up until he was ninety and always worked alone. Bricks that he laid

*Vitis spp. Author's collection.*

as a mason when he was younger are part of the now defunct Burlington Center Mall. From the earnings made after selling his Pineycraft items, he would support extended family who were very poor out of Camden. Henry developed a relationship with buyer Reds Cawley through a love of the Walker coonhound breed that is used for coon hunting. Henry associated Reds with that breed of dog so much that he called Reds "Mr. Walker." Henry was from the poorest, roughest part of Camden, but his work ethic and general kind attitude made him an honorary Piney cut from the same cloth as those Pineys in the heart of Chatsworth. He was loyal to one buyer, whereas many would sell their Pineycraft items to the highest bidder.

His brown station wagon with fake wooden panels had a heavy chain stretched across the hood of the car and a huge padlock at the center. This homemade theft prevention wasn't so someone couldn't steal his car, but at the time, it was common for thieves to steal car batteries. Henry would pull thirty to forty bales every day. To haul that many bales of grapevine, he had the backseats removed and placed a piece of plywood in the back area, extending the space past the opened tailgate. The grapevine was roped down but visible out the back of the modified station wagon.

# PITCH PINECONE

### TOOLS OF THE TRADE

Early on, many different containers were used to collect pinecones. The pickers would use heavy-duty gloves to pull the cone off the tree and put it in the container. They used galvanized tubs in the beginning, but eventually technology caught up, and peach baskets were used with a cord for a handle tied to a person's waist. The larger the container, the harder it was to maneuver around the trees. The first known buyer was Old Man Bucky Roman, located in Whiting, where at his house he would spread the pinecones out in his yard and let the sun open them. This was before there was an Allyn Manufacturing Company Incorporated in Whiting. Allyn had an oven similar to a pizza oven that baked the cones and opened them and was the biggest buyer of pinecones at the time.

*Pinus rigida. Author's collection.*

PERSONAL ACCOUNT

Out of two brothers, Sam, the eldest Lewis brother, loved picking pinecones and would take his brother's son with him. Joe Lewis tells of how the day went:

> *I was about nine or ten years old. We'd drive down the road and get to the plains pretty early and stayed until we got our bags filled. When picking pinecones, one didn't worry about scratches to the side of the truck, as that scrub oak would strip the paint right off. For lunch, Uncle Sam's wife, Lenore, packed us tomato sandwiches with butter. On occasion, when money wasn't tight, we'd stop at the Chesterfield General Store and get German bologna and bread for sandwiches. Now I'd go hungry before I'd eat one of those butter tomato sandwiches, but that's what we had to eat. If we got lucky, we'd get to stop at the only place to get a cold drink or something to eat on the way back from the plains at the Warren Grove Gas Station owned by Anthony and Olga Kato Papszyck and managed and operated by Bill Miller and family.*

In later years, after they closed, a new stop was added. Lucille's Luncheonette served hot coffee and hot chocolate after a cold day on the plains. These instances when Pineys were just coming out of the woods in old ripped clothes that they wore to work in the woods and then going into the public had to create an image to outsiders that these Pineys were wild creatures and somewhat dirty. In reality, they were just coming from a hard day's work.

Little Joe went with his uncle Sam, whom everyone else called Lott, so that he could pay for his school clothes and other items that today we take for granted. Now Joe, who's in his sixties today, recalls one of those times when he went down to the plains and made five dollars working with his uncle Sam. His brother Wayne "Butchy" had stayed home. When Joe got back, his brother told him he found five dollars in an envelope at the New Egypt dump. Boy, little Joe was steamed, as he had to work pretty hard to earn his five dollars with his uncle and here was his brother, who never liked picking pinecones to begin with, loafing around the dump and found five dollars. That's the luck of a Piney.

# GRAY BIRCH: TREES, POLES, WHIPS AND CANDLE HOLDERS

### TOOLS OF THE TRADE

Standard clippers were used to cut young gray birch saplings or, as they called them, birch whips. Birch poles were collected using handsaws. Poles that were thicker in diameter were used for candle holders. The birch poles were measured and cut down using a bench saw that was powered by tractor-belt driven cuts. The Lewises used a truck sometimes to turn the bench saw in Pemberton. The cut pieces were placed in a burlap bag and sold to John Richardson. A saw bench helped keep the house warm by cutting up wood for the stove.

### PERSONAL ACCOUNT

Throughout the state of New Jersey, power lines crisscross the landscape, even in the Pines. One of the best places to cut birch whips was along those power lines that cut through marshy areas. A folk story is that birch whips got their name because the young growth makes a great whip or switch, used at a parent's discretion on a young, unruly child.

In Chatsworth, there was a family of Wills. In the summer, when you drove by their place heading south on Route 72 to Route 563, which bleeds into Main Street Chatsworth, the unofficial capital of the Pines, you could see the yard was filled with drying birch whips. They were only sold without leaves, and the leaves could be beaten off quickly if they were set out in

*Betula populifolia. Author's collection.*

the sun to bake and crumble. Then the Wills family would count them up twenty-five to a bunch. They would pick up a branch and whip a stump or chair until the leaves fell off or use gloved hands to strip the birch of its leaves. A good day's haul could total hundreds of dollars. The high-dollar resale tempted many a Piney to cut them down wherever they found them, regardless of property borders or being on state lands.

## CATTAILS

### TOOLS OF THE TRADE

Cattails were cut along the banks of the rivers that emptied out into the ocean. A corn knife or sickle was used to cut the cattails close to the ground in the dirt with the leaves still on the stalk. Later on, some handpicked the stalks without cutting but instead stripped them by grabbing the stalk of the cattails, grabbing every leaf on the stalk and pulling it apart. That would clean the cattail and leave it ready to be sold. You had to even up bunches with stalks of eighteen inches and cut off extra top growth. They were bundled in 250 each. Also, a ring knife was used by some Pineys for cutting cattails and other smaller-stemmed items like foxtails that wouldn't pull out of their stalks. A rat tail file was used to sharpen it prior to use.

Cattailing has a short season a couple of weeks after Memorial Day. Most of the Pineys in Chatsworth cut cattails in Lower Bank. Other Pineys found them off Route 9 in the Tuckerton area. They parked on the left-hand side of the Lower Bank Bridge and crossed the ditch on the right-hand side or walked out on the left. There was a big barrel out in the meadow like a watch tower. Cattails were thick there. Judd Cawley tells of a place where he and his dad went off San Francisco Road. They had a boat and used it to get to locations those without a boat couldn't reach.

Judd said:

> *Over Lower Bank Bridge, make a left and another left to San Fran, a dirt road that goes out to Landing Creek off of the Mullica River. We took Gordy Lockwood sometimes or others if there was room in the boat throughout the season. Dad and I caught thousands of muskrats and minks also in same area throughout the '70s and '80s before the phragmites started to take over. Both the muskrat and the cattails died out because of the phragmites.*

Judd did some arithmetic and said, "By the end of the 1980s, there were hardly any cattails around, and both the muskrat and mink population went down by a minimum of roughly 85 percent." Muskrat depended on the cattail for food, and the minks depended on muskrat for part of its diet.

*Typha spp. Author's collection.*

One time, Judd, his younger brother Jake and his dad were out on that creek cutting. They were cattailing, and they had thirty-five thousand cattails on the overloaded boat between the three of them. You made the wrong move and the boat would flip. A thunderstorm rolled in, and it was bad; they had to get out of there. They pulled into an old duck blind until it passed. They had to bale water out with a coffee cup when they got safely back to the dock. The boat didn't fare as well. After winching it onto the trailer, with the added water and weight of the cattails, the boat came crashing down, and when it landed it broke the trailer, requiring another trailer to be called in. Judd remembers fondly stories of cutting cattails, as it was a staple in the family budget. He recalls buying his first truck, a 1981 Chevy Deluxe half-ton pickup, with the money collected from cattails using the stripping method.

A funny side note is that back then, the Cawley family wore Chuck Taylor Converse sneakers out in the meadows, as they dried out quickly after getting in the muck of the meadows and they were cheap at the store. Most of the Pineys in that area shopped at the discount store Gregory's of Mount Holly. Reds, the dad, always wore a red pair of Chucks, maybe cause he himself had a head of flaming red hair.

# ATLANTIC WHITE CEDAR: BOXES, CROSSES, POLES AND SLABS

## TOOLS OF THE TRADE

The Richardsons would purchase a truckload of cedar slabs in four-foot sections from a South Jersey sawmill. The boxes were assembled on-site using a table saw to cut the cedar slabs and hammer and nails to assemble the boxes. When used as a planter, a piece of wax paper and sphagnum moss were added to the planter.

## PERSONAL ACCOUNT

One time, the Cawleys were working for Lester Richardson, who at the time was working on his own, separate from his brother John. Lester went out working with Reds. Lester's son Ronnie Richardson and Reds's wife, Alice Cawley, were left behind in a field. It being an extremely hot and humid summer day, Ronnie decided they needed drinks before they started. Alice drove him to the store to pick up a case of cold beer. They

*Chamaecyparis thyoides. Author's collection.*

were out in the sun all day and made five hundred boxes. But drinking beer in the sun working up a sweat wasn't a good idea. Alice said, "The wind was blowing; it was hot. And you know when you're drinking beer in the sun it's not a good thing. I don't know what I thought I saw, but I thought it was some kind of big monster. We were sitting on the ground hammering these cedar slabs together to make boxes. Well, what I was looking at, what I thought was a big monster, later I found out it was only a groundhog. When you're drinking beer in the hot sun, things tend to look a little bit different." The next day, they found out that only a few of the cedar boxes were made correctly and the rest had to be redone. That was Alice's closest brush with the Jersey Devil.

# Bibliography

Anonymous farmer. Personal interview, February 15, 2019.

Antener, Cathy. Personal interview, September 23, 2019.

Berger, Jonathon, and John Walter Sinton. *Water, Earth, and Fire: Land Use and Environmental Planning in the New Jersey Pine Barrens*. Baltimore: Johns Hopkins University Press, 1985.

Bowker, Nancy. "Going Back in Time to the County Fair." *Burlington County Times*, March 14, 1986.

Boyd, Howard P. *A Field Guide to the Pine Barrens of New Jersey*. Medford, NJ: Plexus Publishing, 1991.

*Burlington County Times*. "First Train to '67 Mount Holly Fair." February 13, 1969.

Cawley, Alice. Personal interview, July 4, 2019.

Cawley, Judd. Personal interview, June 21, 2019.

Cloyd, Allison M. "Re: The Best Books I Have Ever Read." E-mail to Emily Gover, July 23, 2014.

Disability History Museum. "Kite, Elizabeth S. The 'Pineys.'" October 4, 1913. www.disabilitymuseum.org/dhm/lib/detail.html?id=2181&&page=all.

Emery, Donald. Personal interview, April 25, 2019.

Faber, Harold. "Gypsy Moth Caused Record Losses in '81 in Northeastern U.S." *New York Times*, August 10, 1981. www.nytimes.com/1981/08/10/nyregion/gypsy-moth-caused-record-losses-in-81-in-northeastern-us.html.

Hingston, Sandy. "13 Things You Might Not Know About the Pine Barrens." *Philly Magazine*, March 2, 2016. www.phillymag.com/news/2016/02/12/pine-barrens-new-jersey/#rQv4IS007GMzBcFA.99.

Hufford, Mary. *One Space, Many Places: Folklife and Land Use in New Jersey's Pinelands National Reserve.* Washington, D.C.: American Folklife Center, Library of Congress, 1986.

Jahn, Robert. *Down Barnegat Bay: A Nor'easter Midnight Reader.* Mantoloking, NJ: Beachcomber Press, 1980.

Janson, Donald. "Ban on Construction Divides Jersey Pine Barrens." *New York Times*, April 5, 1979. www.nytimes.com/1979/04/05/archives/ban-on-construction-divides-jersey-pine-barrens-the-talk-of-the.html.

Jordan, Chris. "Jenni 'JWoww' Farley Interview for *Jersey Shore Massacre* Movie." *Daily Record*, August 24, 2014.

Kite, E. "The Pineys." *The Survey*, 1913.

Lewis, Joseph. Personal interview, March 24, 2019.

Lockwood, Gordy. Personal interview, July 1, 2019.

McDonald, Dennis. Personal interview, April 13, 2020.

McGarvey, Robert G. "The Pine Barrens: Isolation and Image." Master of Arts thesis, Temple University, May 1972.

McPhee, John. *The Pine Barrens.* New York: Farrar, Straus and Giroux, 1968.

Merriam-Webster. "Forage." www.merriam-webster.com/dictionary/forage.

Monteschio, Mary E. "RE: [EXTERNAL] Re: Just a quick hello!" E-mail to William Lewis, February 6, 2019.

Moonsammy, Rita Zorn, David Steven Cohen and Lorraine E. Williams. *Pinelands Folklife.* New Jersey State Council on the Arts, New Jersey Historical Commission, New Jersey State Museum. New Brunswick, NJ: Rutgers University Press, 1987.

Mount Holly, Burlington County, New Jersey. New York: Sanborn Map Company, 1922.

*Mount Holly Herald.* "Gamblers Jittery as Police Dragnet Closes; 10 Nabbed." June 6, 1947.

———. "Jersey Gaining Prominence for Breeding Race Horses." August 8, 1947.

Murray, Charles. *Losing Ground: American Social Policy, 1950–1980.* New York: Basic Books, Inc., 1984.

Myers, William Starr. *The Story of New Jersey.* N.p.: Lewis Historical Publishing Co., Inc., 1945.

New Jersey Gov. "History." www.nj.gov/pinelands/reserve/hist.

New Jersey Pinelands Commission. "Pinelands Facts, Revised 3/27/2020." www.nj.gov/pinelands/infor/fact/Pinelands%20Facts.pdf.

"New Jersey Pinelands Comprehensive Management Plan." Adopted November 21, 1980.

NJ Breds. "About Thoroughbred Breeders' Association of New Jersey." www.njbreds.com/about.

NJ Fish and Wildlife. "The Interstate Wildlife Violator Compact." February 6, 2019. www.njfishandwildlife.com/violators_compact.htm.

NJPineBarrens forum. May 1, 2015.

Ocean Spray. "Our Story Our Heritage." www.oceanspray.com/Our-Story.

Perinchief, Elizabeth M. "Kite Report Was Bad News for Pineland Dwelling." *Batsto Citizens Gazette*, Spring/Summer 1980.

Pic-A-Lilli Inn. "About Pic-A-Lilli Inn." www.picalilli.com/about.

Pinelands Preservation Alliance. "Protection—Pinelands Overview." www.pinelandsalliance.org/protection/overview.

Recreation.gov. "New Jersey Pinelands National Reserve." www.recreation.gov/camping/gateways/2892.

Rich, Eleanor Danser. Personal interview, September 25, 2019.

Richardson, John. Personal interview, February 8, 2019.

Richardson, Pamela. Personal interview, February 14, 2019.

Rozinski, Danielle. *Sounds of the Jersey Pines: The History of the Pinelands Cultural Society*. N.p.: Albert Music Hall, 2019.

Rubinstein, Nora. "A Psycho-Social Impact Analysis of Environmental Change in the New Jersey Pine Barrens." PhD dissertation, University of New York, 1983.

Scheinfeld, A. "The Kallikaks after Thirty Years." *Journal of Heredity*, 1944.

Shinn, Henry. *The History of Mount Holly*. N.p.: Sleeper, 1957.

Shipski, Wess. Personal interview, July 12, 2019.

Smith, John David. *Minds Made Feeble: The Myth and Legacy of the Kallikaks*. Rockville, MD: Aspen Publications, 1985.

Still, Cecil C. *Botany and Healing Medicinal Plants of New Jersey and the Region*. New Brunswick, NJ: Rutgers University Press, 1998.

Tigar, Lawrence. Personal interview, March 25, 2019.

U.S. Highbush Blueberry Council. "History of Blueberries." www.blueberrycouncil.org/about-blueberries/history-of-blueberries.

Valenza, Samuel W., Jr. *The Secret Casino at Red Men's Hall*. Bloomington, IN: iUniverse LLC, 1995.

Wasiowich, Bill. Personal interview, May 4, 2020.

Wikipedia. "1950s American Automobile Culture." en.wikipedia.org/wiki/1950s_American_automobile_culture.

———. "Phillies (cigar)." en.wikipedia.org/w/index.php?title=Phillies_(cigar)&oldid=896268284.

————. "Piney (Pine Barrens resident)." en.wikipedia.org/wiki/Piney_ (Pine_Barrens_resident).

YouTube. "FDR's Tree Army: The Civilian Conservation Corps." December 27, 2017. www.youtube.com.

————. "New Jersey Folk Festival Archive." September 27, 2015. www. youtube.com.

# About the Author

Willilliam J. Lewis is a lifetime resident of the New Jersey Pine Barrens, as were multiple generations of his family before him. He shares his Piney adventures on social media networks under "Piney Tribe." He preaches exploration without exploitation and to teach our children to be tomorrow's environmental stewards. After proudly serving as a United States Marine, William went on to graduate from Rider University. He founded an environmental nonprofit to get kids outdoors and has served in leadership roles for both governmental and New Jersey nonprofit organizations. His travel mileage stretches across the globe from many locations in the United States to the Horn of Africa, which has helped in enriching his perspective of our New Jersey Pine Barrens.